"In the end, only three things matter: how much you loved, how gently you lived, and how gracefully you let go of things not meant for you."

Buddha

Zen Stories Inspired by Principles of Buddhism, Taoism, and Ikigai

DISCLAIMER

THE AUTHOR AND PUBLISHER HAVE MADE EVERY EFFORT TO ENSURE THESE TALES ARE AS ACCURATE, ENTERTAINING, AND ENLIGHTENING AS A MONK'S SERENE SMILE AFTER A DEEP MEDITATION SESSION. BUT, AS WITH ALL THINGS IN LIFE (AND ESPECIALLY WITH STORIES THAT HAVE BEEN AROUND LONGER THAN YOUR GREAT-GREAT-GREAT-GRANDPARENT), SOME DETAILS MIGHT HAVE BEEN LOST, EMBELLISHED, OR MAY HAVE TAKEN A DETOUR THROUGH THE MYSTICAL REALM OF INTERPRETATION. IF YOU FIND YOURSELF DEBATING THE PROFOUND MEANINGS, FANTASTIC! BUT REMEMBER, NO TWO JOURNEYS ARE THE SAME; YOURS MIGHT JUST INVOLVE MORE COFFEE AND FEWER LOTUS POSITIONS.

LASTLY, WHILE WE WOULD LOVE FOR YOU TO EMBARK ON A QUEST FOR ENLIGHTENMENT AFTER READING THIS, PLEASE DO SO RESPONSIBLY. DON'T SELL ALL YOUR BELONGINGS AND HEAD TO THE HIMALAYAS WITHOUT PACKING A SWEATER; IT GETS CHILLY UP THERE!

ALL CONTENT IN THIS BOOK IS PROTECTED BY COPYRIGHT LAW. NO PART OF THIS BOOK MAY BE REPRODUCED, DISTRIBUTED, OR TRANSMITTED IN ANY FORM OR BY ANY MEANS, INCLUDING PHOTOCOPYING, RECORDING, OR OTHER ELECTRONIC OR MECHANICAL METHODS, WITHOUT THE PRIOR WRITTEN PERMISSION OF THE AUTHOR.

THIS BOOK IS INTENDED FOR ENTERTAINMENT, INFORMATIONAL, AND EDUCATIONAL PURPOSES ONLY. THE CONTENT WITHIN IS NOT A SUBSTITUTE FOR PROFESSIONAL ADVICE, WHETHER MEDICAL, LEGAL, OR OTHERWISE. READERS SHOULD EXERCISE THEIR OWN DISCRETION AND JUDGMENT. ALL PRACTICES AND ACTIVITIES DESCRIBED ARE FICTIONAL AND SHOULD NOT BE USED TO CAUSE HARM TO ONESELF OR OTHERS. THE AUTHOR AND PUBLISHER ARE NOT RESPONSIBLE FOR ANY OUTCOMES RESULTING FROM THE USE OF THE INFORMATION PROVIDED.

ANY UNAUTHORIZED USE OF THE CONTENT IN THIS BOOK IS STRICTLY PROHIBITED AND MAY RESULT IN LEGAL ACTION.
ALL RIGHTS RESERVED © 2024

Contents

INTRODUCTION TO BUDDHISM 7
THE IMPORTANCE OF STORYTELLING AND PARABLES IN BUDDHISM 9
INTRODUCTION TO TAOISM 12
INTRODUCTION TO IKIGAI 22
MONEY AND WEALTH - ILLUSIONS OF ABUNDANCE 31

    The Gold Leaf and the Banyan Tree 36
    The Merchant's Greatest Treasure 39
    The Echoing Caverns of Sariputra 42
    The Labyrinth of Desires 45
    The Enigma of Shattered Mirrors 48
    The Garden of Fleeting Shadows 51
    The Maze of Temptation 54
    The Unyielding Tree and the Whispering Breeze 57
    The Mirror Lake of Sati 60
    The Golden Cage of Sunyata 63
    The Silken Thread of Samadhi 65
    The Currency of Stillness 68
    The Resonance of True Desires 71
    The Unseen Garden of Dukkha 73
    The Silver Coin's Journey 76
    The Symphony of Silhouettes 79
    The Tapestry of Dreams 82

Karma and the Law of Cause and Effect 85
- The Orchard of Choices 92
- The Unseen Balance 95
- The Pottery of Fate 98
- The Enigma of Lushan's Bridge 101
- Niraya's Enchanted Garden 104
- The Dance of the Celestial Lotus 107
- The Golden Scales of Jivana 109
- The Chained Chalice of Vimukti 112
- The Reflective Orchard of Padma 114
- The River of Samsara 117
- The Symphony of Cosmic Echoes 120
- The Garden of Imprints 123

The Ego and Humility 126
- The Lake of Mirrored Souls 132
- The Bamboo and the Oak 135
- The Ego and the Essence 138
- The Mountain and the Grain of Sand 141
- The Weaver and the King 144
- The Tale of the Silent Mountain 147
- The Feather and the Stone 150
- The Tale of the Sun and the Moon 153
- The Orchid and the Oak 156
- The Stone Cutter's Desire 159

Acceptance of Change 162

The Dance of the Willow Tree 168
The Unyielding Stone and the Gentle Stream 171
The Tale of the Blossom and the Breeze 174
The Meeting of Flow and Solidity 177
The Flowing River of Change 180
The Dance of the Everchanging Leaf 183
The Transient Garden 186
The Loom of Time 188
The Seasons of Serenity 190

THE QUEST FOR INNER PEACE 193
Ripples of Clarity 198
Beneath the Veil of the Eternal Moon 201
The Melody of Unheard Strings 203
Journey to the Heart's Silent Chamber 205
The Symphony of Unseen Breezes 208
Beneath the Veil of Illusions 211
Whispers of the Bamboo Grove 214
The Paradox of Inner Stillness 217
Silence Beyond the Murmurs 220

THE BALANCE OF WORK AND REST 223
The Harmony of Effort and Ease 228
Weaving the Fabric of Life 231
Bhima's Path to Equilibrium 234
The Cosmic Dance of Duty and Dream 237
The Tale of Two Dancers 240

Forgiveness and Letting Go 243
The Unseen Anchor of Anila 248
Blossoms of the Unburdened Heart 251
The Cavern of Grudges 254
The Unseen Chains of Viparyaya Valley 256
The Sacred Saga of Serenity 259
The Weightless Pebble 262
The Dancing Shadows of Raya 265
The Ember's Glow 268

The Power of Gratitude 271
The Blooms of Thankfulness 277
Journey to the Heart of Dawn 280
The Songbird's Serenade 283
The Oasis of Appreciation 286
The Lioness and the Elephant 289

INTRODUCTION TO BUDDHISM

In a land where mighty rivers narrate tales of old, cradled by majestic mountains that touch the heavens, a gentle whisper emerged—a whisper that grew into a philosophy, softly calling out to every listening heart. This is the story of Buddhism.

Imagine a palace, its golden walls reflecting brilliance in every corner. Within these walls was a young prince whose life was much like a carefully curated painting—beautiful but limited to its frame. Yet, as is the nature of curiosity, the prince stepped beyond these walls one day and saw life in its unfiltered form: the frailty of age, the pain of sickness, and the inevitable shadow of death. These sights, foreign to his protected existence, stirred a deep quest within him to understand life's true essence.

This prince's journey is not just a tale of ages gone by but an echo of the questions we all harbor deep within. After years of introspection, beneath a tree that witnessed his transformation, the prince gleaned truths about life's sorrows and the path to rise above them. These revelations became the cornerstones of Buddhism: a realization of life's inherent suffering and a guide on how to transcend it.

However, the beauty of this philosophy isn't restricted to a single revelation. Like a river that branches and expands, touching various lands and civilizations, Buddhism flowed

and evolved. From understanding life's middle path—avoiding extremes of both deprivation and excess—it delved into the profound realization of 'emptiness.' But worry not, for this 'emptiness' is not a bleak void. Instead, think of it as a canvas, brimming with potential, ready to be painted with the colors of experience, understanding that everything is interconnected and nothing exists in isolation.

As this philosophy journeyed further, touching different shores, it took on new forms and practices. Yet, at its heart remained a simple and profound message: an invitation to look within, to understand oneself deeply, and through this understanding, attain a peace that transcends worldly turmoil.

For you, dear reader, who might be taking the first steps into this vast ocean of wisdom, let this narrative be a gentle hand guiding you through the currents. It's not just a historical account but a journey for the soul, an exploration of questions that have haunted humanity since time immemorial, and the answers that have the potential to liberate. Dive in with an open heart and a curious mind, and let the waves of Buddhism wash over you, leaving you transformed and enlightened.

The Importance of Storytelling and Parables in Buddhism

In the vast expanse of human existence, where moments become memories and memories fade into the abyss of time, stories emerge as bridges, connecting past to present, wisdom to understanding, and soul to soul. The tapestry of Buddhism, intricate and beautiful, is woven with these threads of tales and parables, guiding countless hearts toward enlightenment.

Imagine, for a moment, the tranquility of a serene pond, its waters undisturbed. Now, envision a single pebble dropped into its midst. The impact, though gentle, sends ripples across the surface, touching every corner. In a similar essence, stories and parables within Buddhism function as these pebbles, causing ripples of understanding in the calm waters of our minds.

You see, their complexity often veils the profundity of life's truths. To dive deep into the realms of existence, morality, and consciousness might appear daunting for many. Herein lies the beauty of storytelling: it simplifies without diluting; it enlightens without overwhelming. By weaving wisdom into narratives, the abstract becomes tangible, the profound becomes relatable, and the teachings become accessible.

Consider parables as gentle guides. In a forest dense with the foliage of doubt, parables light up the path, revealing the

way with clarity. They are mirrors, reflecting back to us not just the external world but the intricacies of our inner selves. They prompt introspection, provoke thought, and foster understanding. They speak not in commands but in suggestions, allowing each seeker to derive personal insights and revelations.

The voyage of Buddhism from its inception to its myriad forms today has been colored with countless narratives. These stories serve a dual purpose, whether of a compassionate Bodhisattva aiding a suffering being or of a monk realizing the truth after witnessing a falling leaf. Firstly, they immortalize the timeless wisdom of the enlightened ones, ensuring that their insights are not lost in the sands of time. Secondly, they function as beacons, drawing seekers towards the core principles of Buddhism, making the journey less about rote learning and more about experiential understanding.

Envision a secret garden, bathed in the soft glow of twilight. Every tale in this book blossoms like a rare, radiant flower, eager to whisper its secrets to the winds. As you wander through this enchanted haven, linger beside each bloom. Let its alluring aroma wrap around you, guiding you on a dance through worlds of serenity and profound wisdom.

To the novice, just beginning to dip their toes into this vast ocean, stories, and parables will be your companions. They will laugh with you in moments of joy, comfort you in times

of doubt, and illuminate your path when shadows of uncertainty loom. Let your heart be open, let your mind be receptive, for in the world of Buddhist storytelling, every tale is a step towards enlightenment, every parable a bridge to understanding. Embrace them, reflect upon them, and let them guide you on this wondrous journey of discovery.

INTRODUCTION TO TAOISM

In the heart of ancient China, a profound and serene philosophy emerged, guiding individuals toward a harmonious way of life. This philosophy is Taoism, a tradition that emphasizes harmony with the Tao, the fundamental essence of the universe. Tao, often translated as "The Way," represents the underlying essence that flows through all things, binding the universe in a seamless, dynamic balance.

Taoism encourages us to embrace simplicity, cultivate inner peace, and live in accordance with the natural order. It teaches that true wisdom and contentment arise from understanding and aligning oneself with the rhythms of nature. This introduction will explore the essential principles of Taoism and how they can be integrated into our daily lives.

UNDERSTANDING THE TAO

The Tao is an enigmatic concept, often described as indefinable and ineffable. It is the source of all existence, the ultimate reality that transcends human comprehension. The Tao is not a deity but a principle that underlies the cosmos, guiding the natural order. To understand the Tao, one must look beyond the superficial and embrace the subtleties of life.

The Tao Te Ching, traditionally credited to the sage Lao Tzu, is one of the most important texts in Taoism. It offers profound insights into the nature of the Tao and how to live

in accordance with it. The text emphasizes the importance of wu wei, or effortless action. This principle teaches that by aligning with the Tao, one can achieve more by doing less. It is about flowing with the currents of life rather than struggling against them.

THE PRINCIPLE OF WU WEI

Wu wei is a core principle in Taoism, often translated as "non-action" or "effortless action." It does not imply laziness or inactivity but rather a state of being in which actions arise spontaneously and harmoniously from one's connection with the Tao. When we practice wu wei, we act in accordance with the natural flow of life, avoiding force and resistance.

This principle is elegantly demonstrated in the story of "The Unyielding Tree and the Whispering Breeze" in this book, where the tree stands firm yet flexible, bending with the breeze without breaking. This story reflects the Taoist belief that strength comes from yielding and that true power lies in gentleness and adaptability.

THE BALANCE OF YIN AND YANG

Another fundamental principle of Taoism is the balance of yin and yang, the complementary forces that create harmony in the universe. Yin represents the passive, receptive, and nurturing aspects of life, while yang embodies the active,

assertive, and creative forces. Taoism teaches that these forces are interdependent and that balance between them leads to a harmonious existence.

In the story "The Garden of Fleeting Shadows," we see the interplay of light and shadow, symbolizing the dynamic balance of yin and yang. The characters learn that embracing both aspects of life, rather than seeking to eliminate one in favor of the other, leads to true harmony and peace.

SIMPLICITY AND CONTENTMENT

Taoism values simplicity and contentment, advocating for a life free from excessive desires and complexities. It inspires us to discover happiness in the simplicity of everyday moments and to appreciate the natural beauty around us. This philosophy aligns with the story "The Currency of Stillness," where the protagonist discovers peace and fulfillment in a life of simplicity and mindfulness.

By letting go of unnecessary attachments and desires, we can cultivate a state of inner tranquility. Taoism teaches that true happiness comes not from external achievements or possessions but from within, through a deep connection with the Tao.

LIVING IN HARMONY WITH NATURE

Nature holds a sacred place in Taoism, seen as a reflection of the Tao itself. Taoist practices often involve spending time in natural settings, observing the rhythms of the seasons, and living in accordance with the natural world. This reverence for nature is evident in the story "The Gold Leaf and the Banyan Tree," where the characters find wisdom and solace in their connection with the natural environment.

Taoism encourages us to live sustainably, respecting the earth and its resources. By attuning ourselves to the cycles of nature, we can cultivate a more balanced and harmonious life.

PRACTICAL STEPS TO EMBRACE TAOISM

1. **Mindfulness and Meditation**: Practice mindfulness and meditation to cultivate a deep awareness of the present moment. This helps to align with the Tao and fosters a state of wu wei.
2. **Simplify Your Life**: Focus on simplifying your life by reducing material possessions and unnecessary distractions. Appreciate the elegance of simplicity and find joy in the small things.
3. **Connect with Nature**: Spend time in nature, observing its rhythms and cycles. Let nature be your guide and teacher, helping you to understand the principles of yin and yang.

4. **Embrace Flexibility**: Adopt a flexible mindset, allowing yourself to adapt to changing circumstances without resistance. Remember that true strength lies in being able to yield and bend like the tree in the breeze.
5. **Seek Balance**: Aim for balance in all aspects of your life. Acknowledge the significance of both yin and yang, and work towards harmonizing these forces within yourself and your surroundings.

APPLYING TAOIST PRINCIPLES IN MODERN LIFE

INTRODUCTION TO PRACTICAL APPLICATION

Integrating Taoist principles into your daily routine can foster a more balanced, harmonious, and rewarding life existence. In this part, we will explore actionable strategies for applying Taoist wisdom to various aspects of modern life, including work, relationships, health, and personal growth.

EMBRACING WU WEI IN DAILY LIFE

The principle of *wu wei*, or the practice of effortless action, lies at the heart of Taoism. It teaches us to align our actions in harmony with life's natural flow, letting things unfold without unnecessary force or struggle.

WU WEI AT WORK

Applying wu wei at work involves finding ways to flow with the tasks at hand rather than forcing outcomes. It means working efficiently and harmoniously, maintaining a balance between effort and ease.

- Exercise: Identify tasks at work where you feel the most resistance or stress. Reflect on how you can approach these tasks more naturally and with less force. Practice taking short breaks to reset your mind and return to work with a fresh perspective.

WU WEI IN RELATIONSHIPS

In relationships, wu wei encourages us to interact with others naturally and authentically, without trying to control or manipulate outcomes. It highlights the value of listening, empathy, and spontaneous interaction.

- Exercise: Practice active listening in your interactions. Focus on being fully present with the other person, allowing conversations to flow naturally. Refrain from interrupting or trying to steer the conversation; instead, respond authentically and intuitively.

Cultivating Yin-Yang Balance

The dynamic interplay of yin and yang is crucial for preserving harmony in all aspects of life. Achieving balance between these complementary forces can enhance well-being and inner peace.

Balancing Yin and Yang in Health

In health, balance is achieved by harmonizing rest (yin) and activity (yang), diet, and emotional states. Recognizing when you need more of one energy than the other can lead to better health and vitality.

- Exercise: Create a daily routine that includes both yin and yang activities. For instance, balance periods of intense physical activity with restorative practices like meditation or gentle stretching. Pay attention to your diet, balancing light, cooling foods (yin) with warming, energizing foods (yang).

Balancing Yin and Yang in Personal Growth

Personal growth involves both introspection (yin) and action (yang). Finding equilibrium among these aspects can lead to meaningful progress and self-awareness.

- Exercise: Dedicate time each week for self-reflection and goal setting. Utilize journaling as a tool to delve

into your thoughts and feelings (yin) and create actionable plans to achieve your goals (yang). Regularly review and adjust your balance as needed.

SIMPLICITY AND CONTENTMENT

Taoism advocates for simplicity and contentment, encouraging us to find joy in the simple things and to let go of excessive desires and complications.

SIMPLIFYING YOUR ENVIRONMENT

Creating a simple, uncluttered environment can promote tranquility and focus, making it easier to connect with the Tao.

- Exercise: Spend time decluttering your living and working spaces. Eliminate items that no longer have a purpose and organize your surroundings to promote calm and clarity. Adopt a minimalist approach, keeping only what is essential and meaningful.

FINDING CONTENTMENT IN EVERYDAY LIFE

Contentment arises from appreciating the present moment and finding joy in simple pleasures. Practicing gratitude can help cultivate this state of mind.

- Exercise: Begin a daily gratitude practice. Each evening, write down three things you are grateful for

that day, focusing on simple, everyday experiences. Reflect on how these moments contribute to your overall sense of contentment and well-being.

Connecting with Nature

Nature holds a sacred place in Taoism, serving as a mirror of the Tao and a source of wisdom and inspiration. Spending time in natural settings can help us reconnect with the rhythms of life and deepen our understanding of the Tao.

Nature as a Teacher

Observing nature can provide profound insights into the principles of yin and yang, wu wei, and the interconnectedness of all things.

- Exercise: Take regular walks in nature-rich environments like parks, forests, or near bodies of water. During your walks, practice mindfulness by noticing the sights, sounds, and sensations around you. Reflect on how the natural world embodies the principles of Taoism.

Sustainable Living

Living in harmony with nature also involves adopting sustainable practices that respect and preserve the environment.

- Exercise: Evaluate your lifestyle and identify areas where you can reduce your environmental impact. This might include reducing waste, conserving energy, and choosing sustainable products. Make small, incremental changes to align your habits with the principles of sustainability.

INTRODUCTION TO IKIGAI

In the serene and timeless villages of Okinawa, Japan, lies a profound secret to a long, fulfilling life, quietly flourishing in the heart of its culture and daily practices. This secret is Ikigai, a term that translates to "a reason for being." Ikigai is more than just a word; it is a philosophy that intertwines what you love, what you are good at, what the world needs, and what you can be paid for into a harmonious and meaningful existence.

THE ESSENCE OF IKIGAI

Ikigai is not a fleeting trend but a deeply ingrained cultural concept that has been nurtured over generations in Okinawa. This region is renowned for its unusually high concentration of centenarians — individuals who live to be over 100 years old. Researchers and scholars have studied these centenarians extensively, uncovering that their secret to longevity and happiness lies in their Ikigai.

Unlike the often hectic and fast-paced life experienced in many parts of the world, the Okinawans live with a profound sense of purpose. Each day is approached with mindfulness and intention, fostering a deep connection to the activities and people around them. Whether it is tending to their lush gardens, engaging in traditional crafts, participating in community festivals, or just simply enjoying a meal with loved

ones, the Okinawans find joy and meaning in the simplicity of everyday life.

THE FOUNDATION OF IKIGAI

At the heart of Ikigai are four essential components that create a balanced and fulfilling life:

1. ***What You Love (Passion):*** *This is the element that brings you joy and excitement. It encompasses activities and pursuits that ignite your spirit and make you feel truly alive. Engaging in what you love can transform mundane moments into cherished experiences, infusing your life with enthusiasm and zest.*
2. ***What You Are Good At (Profession):*** *These are your unique skills and talents that you have honed over time. When you utilize these abilities, you not only achieve a sense of accomplishment but also contribute to your personal and professional growth. Mastery in your chosen field can lead to a deeper sense of self-worth and satisfaction.*
3. ***What the World Needs (Mission):*** *This aspect emphasizes the importance of contributing to society and making a positive impact on the world around you. It involves understanding the needs of others and finding ways to address them through your actions. Fulfilling this component brings a sense of purpose that extends beyond personal gratification.*

4. **What You Can Be Paid For (Vocation):** This ensures that you can sustain yourself financially while pursuing your passions and skills. It is about finding a career or occupation that not only supports your livelihood but also aligns with your interests and values. Achieving this balance allows you to thrive both economically and personally.

THE JOURNEY TO DISCOVERING IKIGAI

The journey to discovering your Ikigai is deeply personal and unique to each individual. It requires introspection, exploration, and a willingness to embrace change. While the path may not always be straightforward, the pursuit of Ikigai promises profound rewards.

SELF-REFLECTION

The first step towards uncovering your Ikigai is self-reflection. Spend time contemplating your passions, interests, and what truly brings you joy. Consider the activities that make you lose track of time, those moments when you feel fully engaged and alive. Reflect on your strengths and the skills you have developed over the years. Journaling can be an effective tool in this journey, enabling you to record your thoughts and uncover patterns in your experiences.

EXPERIMENT AND EXPLORE

After identifying your passions and strengths, the next step is to experiment and explore. Do not be afraid to try new activities or revisit old hobbies. Enroll in classes that interest you, such as painting, cooking, or learning a new language. Volunteer for causes that resonate with you. This exploration phase is crucial for discovering what resonates with you and aligns with your Ikigai.

SEEK FEEDBACK

Engage in discussions with friends, family, and colleagues to gain insights into your strengths and unique contributions. Sometimes, others can see qualities in us that we may overlook. Seek feedback about the times they have seen you at your best and what they believe you excel at. This external perspective can provide valuable clues in your journey to finding Ikigai.

ALIGN WITH VALUES

Ensure that your pursuits align with your core values and beliefs. Reflect on what principles are most important to you and how they can guide your actions. When your activities and goals are in harmony with your values, you are more likely to experience lasting satisfaction and fulfillment.

Integrate and Adjust

Discovering your Ikigai is not a one-time event but an ongoing process of integration and adjustment. Look for ways to incorporate your Ikigai into your daily routine. This might mean making small changes to how you spend your time or even considering a career change if necessary. The key is to remain open to new possibilities and be willing to adapt as you grow and evolve.

Living Your Ikigai

Living your Ikigai means embracing a lifestyle that fosters continuous engagement and satisfaction. It involves staying active, being involved in your community, and finding joy in the small things. The pillars of Ikigai include starting small, releasing yourself from unnecessary burdens, finding harmony and sustainability, enjoying the little things, and being present in the moment.

By embracing these principles, you can cultivate a lasting sense of fulfillment and happiness. The journey to finding and living your Ikigai is a path worth taking, filled with moments of discovery, joy, and profound satisfaction. Each step brings you closer to a life rich with purpose and meaning, just as it has for the centenarians of Okinawa.

IKIGAI AND THE PERSONAL DEVELOPMENT RENAISSANCE

Ikigai, while rooted in tradition, serves as a framework for personal development in today's fast-paced world. Beyond its cultural origins, it provides tools and perspectives that revolutionize how individuals approach self-growth and fulfillment.

1. The Self-Discovery Revolution

Modern personal development often focuses on external achievements, but Ikigai encourages a deeper, inward journey. It challenges individuals to:

- Identify their "why" by reflecting on their passions and purpose.
- Explore forgotten dreams and rekindle dormant talents.
- Reevaluate life goals to ensure alignment with inner values rather than societal pressures.

This shift towards introspection enables people to design a life that genuinely resonates with their true selves.

2. Emotional Mastery through Ikigai

Ikigai emphasizes harmony not just with others but within oneself. Emotional mastery becomes a natural byproduct of living in alignment with this philosophy:

- **Mindful Presence:** By focusing on what brings joy and meaning, individuals cultivate gratitude and reduce emotional turbulence.
- **Resilience Building:** Knowing one's Ikigai helps to contextualize setbacks as temporary and purposeful challenges.
- **Positive Emotional Cycles:** Engaging in meaningful activities creates cycles of fulfillment and happiness, reinforcing emotional stability.

3. Designing a Purpose-Driven Daily Routine

Ikigai is inherently practical. It provides a roadmap for structuring daily life around meaningful activities:

- **Morning Intentions:** Begin each day by revisiting your Ikigai, setting small goals that align with your greater purpose.
- **Micro Ikigai Moments:** Incorporate simple, fulfilling actions—a walk in nature, a moment of creativity, or a meaningful conversation—into your daily routine.
- **Reflection Practices:** Conclude the day by reflecting on how well your activities aligned with your Ikigai and how you can adjust tomorrow.

IKIGAI AS A CATALYST FOR SKILL MASTERY

1. Leveraging Passion for Lifelong Learning

Ikigai motivates individuals to embrace lifelong learning as a journey of joy and purpose. This approach transforms learning from a task into an enriching experience:

- Pursue skills that genuinely excite you rather than those dictated by external pressures.
- Embrace curiosity and experimentation as ways to discover hidden talents.
- Reframe mistakes as stepping stones towards mastery.

2. Creating Synergy Between Skills and Purpose

Ikigai enables individuals to identify intersections between their skills and their greater purpose. By aligning professional aspirations with personal passions, people create careers that feel like extensions of their true selves.

3. Expanding Creative Potential

Ikigai unlocks creativity by encouraging people to:

- Combine unrelated skills and interests to create unique solutions.
- Take risks in exploring new hobbies or professional paths.
- Collaborate with others who share their values and purpose.

Ikigai's Role in Mental and Physical Well-Being

1. Stress Reduction through Purposeful Living

A clear sense of purpose reduces stress by providing clarity and focus. People who live in alignment with their Ikigai often:

- Avoid unnecessary commitments that detract from their purpose.
- Cultivate mindfulness through activities they love.
- Experience fewer stress-related health issues, as seen in Okinawa's centenarians.

2. Energizing the Body through Meaningful Activities

Physical activity becomes more sustainable when it aligns with one's purpose. Whether it's gardening, dancing, or martial arts, Ikigai encourages individuals to:

- Engage in enjoyable physical activities that contribute to their sense of fulfillment.
- Prioritize health not as an obligation but as a means to pursue their passions.

3. Promoting Longevity Through Joy

The Okinawan lifestyle shows how Ikigai directly correlates with longevity. The joy derived from living with purpose fuels mental and physical vitality, contributing to longer and healthier lives.

Money and Wealth - Illusions of Abundance

In a world that often equates success and happiness with material wealth, it is easy to fall into the trap of believing that more money and possessions will bring lasting satisfaction. However, the pursuit of wealth can lead to a perpetual cycle of desire and discontent, obscuring the true sources of fulfillment and happiness. Yet, the tales in this chapter unveil deeper truths, weaving through the principles of Buddhism, Taoism, and Ikigai to reveal the true essence of abundance beyond material wealth.

The Illusory Nature of Wealth

Money and material possessions are often seen as symbols of success and happiness. Yet, countless studies and personal experiences show that beyond a certain point, increased wealth does not equate to greater happiness. In fact, the relentless pursuit of money can lead to stress, anxiety, and a never-ending cycle of desire.

In modern society, the illusion of abundance is perpetuated by consumer culture, which encourages constant accumulation and equates material possessions with personal worth. This mindset can lead to a sense of emptiness and dissatisfaction, as the temporary pleasure derived from acquiring new things quickly fades, leaving a void that demands to be filled with even more consumption.

Buddhism: The Impermanence of Wealth

Buddhism teaches that attachment to material wealth is a source of suffering. The concept of *anicca* (impermanence) reminds us that all things, including wealth, are transient and subject to change. By recognizing the impermanent nature of material possessions, we can reduce our attachment to them and find true contentment within ourselves.

In "The Merchant's Greatest Treasure," the protagonist learns that true wealth lies not in his accumulated riches but in the joy of giving and the relationships he fosters. This mirrors the Buddhist teaching that generosity and compassion lead to lasting happiness, while attachment to wealth leads to suffering.

"The Unseen Garden of Dukkha" further illustrates this concept by showing characters who are trapped in a cycle of desire and dissatisfaction, ultimately finding peace through detachment and inner reflection. These tales highlight the Buddhist understanding that letting go of material desires can lead to deeper fulfillment and serenity.

Taoism: Harmony Beyond Materialism

Taoism emphasizes living in harmony with the Tao, the natural way of the universe. It teaches that true wealth lies in simplicity, balance, and inner peace rather than in material accumulation. Taoist philosophy encourages us to seek

contentment within ourselves and in our connection to the natural world, rather than in external possessions.

"The Echoing Caverns of Sariputra" illustrates this Taoist principle beautifully. Characters in the story find that by letting go of their material desires and living simply, they achieve a profound sense of peace and harmony. This reflects the Taoist ideal that true abundance is found in a life of simplicity and connection with nature, rather than in the pursuit of wealth.

"The Garden of Fleeting Shadows" also emphasizes the importance of living in the moment and appreciating the beauty of the natural world. This story reflects the Taoist belief that peace and contentment come from a harmonious existence, free from the relentless pursuit of material gains.

Ikigai: Purpose Beyond Prosperity

Ikigai, the Japanese concept of finding one's reason for being, integrates the idea that true fulfillment comes from living a life of purpose rather than accumulating wealth. When we align our actions with our passions, talents, and the needs of the world, we find a deeper sense of satisfaction that transcends material wealth.

In "The Reflective Orchard of Padma," a character discovers that his true calling lies in nurturing an orchard and sharing its fruits with his community. This story demonstrates that living with purpose and contributing to the well-being of others brings a more profound and lasting

happiness than the pursuit of material wealth. The principle of Ikigai teaches us that true prosperity is found in meaningful actions and a balanced life.

"The Silver Coin's Journey" further illustrates this by showing a character who realizes that the value of his coin lies not in its material worth but in the joy, it can bring to others. This story encapsulates the Ikigai principle that true fulfillment comes from purposeful living and the positive impact we have on those around us.

THE GOLD LEAF AND THE BANYAN TREE

In a small village nestled beside a serene river, a woman named Ananda came into possession of a shimmering gold leaf. It was a rare treasure, much desired by many. Word quickly spread about Ananda's newfound wealth, and soon enough, villagers began to visit her, praising her fortune and showering her with admiration.

But Ananda, influenced by the whispers of society, grew obsessed with her gold leaf. She built a glass case for it, placed it on a pedestal in the middle of her house, and spent hours every day simply gazing at its brilliance. She stopped visiting the riverside, she stopped enjoying the songs of the birds, and she ceased attending community gatherings. In all its glowing grandeur, the gold leaf had become the center of Ananda's universe.

One day, while Ananda was away, a thief entered her house, shattering the glass case and making away with the gold leaf.

When Ananda returned and found her prized possession gone, she was devastated. The loss bore heavily on her heart, and she confined herself to her home, refusing to see anyone.

A week passed, and a wise old monk named Maitreya visited the village. Hearing of Ananda's sorrow, he decided to meet her. He found Ananda, her eyes swollen and red, sitting in the midst of shattered glass, staring at the empty pedestal.

Without uttering a word, Maitreya took Ananda by the hand and led her to a massive banyan tree outside the village. They sat under its vast canopy, feeling the gentle breeze and listening to the rustling of the leaves.

After a long silence, Maitreya spoke, "Ananda, this banyan tree has been here for centuries. It has provided shade to countless generations, its branches a home to numerous birds, and its roots have held firm against countless storms. Yet, the tree doesn't boast about its strength or its age. It simply exists, doing its part for the world."

Ananda, tears streaming down her face, replied, "But Master, the pain of losing my gold leaf is unbearable. It was everything to me."

Maitreya gently responded, "Ananda, it's not the gold leaf you miss, but the value you assigned to it. Like this banyan tree, find value in being and giving rather than possessing. The tree doesn't need gold to be invaluable."

Conclusion:

In our pursuit of material wealth, we often forget the inherent value of existence and being. The banyan tree stands as a testament to the strength and value that comes from simply being, from playing our part in the grand design of the universe. Money and possessions can offer temporary pleasure, but true fulfillment arises when we understand our intrinsic worth, irrespective of external validations. The challenge is to shift our perspective from amassing wealth to enriching our souls and the world around us.

THE MERCHANT'S GREATEST TREASURE

Deep in the heart of the bustling city of Magadha was a successful merchant named Kavi. His vast wealth was known throughout the land, and traders traveled from distant cities to witness the splendor of his abode and do business with him. The walls of his mansion glittered with gold, and the scent of exotic perfumes permeated the air. Every aspect of Kavi's life was bathed in opulence.

Yet, Kavi's sleep was always restless. Despite the riches that surrounded him, a void persisted deep within his heart. One day, after a particularly disturbing dream where he found himself penniless and destitute, Kavi decided to embark on a journey to find the secret to genuine fulfillment.

He traveled through dense forests and scaled high mountains, seeking sages and monks who could shed light on his inner turmoil. One evening, while meditating under a sacred Bodhi tree, Kavi was approached by a hermit with piercing eyes and an aura of tranquility.

"Disturbed by wealth and yet bound by it, aren't you?" whispered the hermit without waiting for an introduction.

Kavi, taken aback, nodded, "Every coin I possess weighs heavily on my soul. Yet, the fear of parting with them cripples me. Tell me, wise one, how do I find peace?"

The hermit beckoned Kavi closer and whispered, "Your journey is not to shed your wealth but to discover its true purpose. Tomorrow, visit the village by the river and seek the woman with the golden loom."

The following dawn, Kavi arrived at the village and soon found the woman. Her loom was indeed gold, but instead of threads, she wove stories—stories of love, compassion, sacrifice, and wisdom. With every tale she told, the eyes of the villagers lit up, their hearts buoyed by hope and purpose.

Kavi approached her and asked, "Why do you weave such tales on a golden loom?"

The woman replied, "The gold is merely a tool, Kavi. It's the stories, the lessons, and the emotions they evoke that are the real treasures. Gold in itself is neutral; it's the purpose we give it that defines its value."

Conclusion:

The tale of Kavi underscores the often-misunderstood concept of wealth in our lives. Money, in its essence, is just a tool—a neutral entity. It's neither good nor bad. Its value arises from the purpose we assign to it. True fulfillment doesn't come from hoarding wealth but from leveraging it for greater purposes—be it spreading wisdom, supporting people in need, or igniting hope. The real challenge lies in shifting our mindset from wealth as a means of power and prestige to viewing it as a tool for positive change and purposeful living.

THE ECHOING CAVERNS OF SARIPUTRA

In ancient Bharat's vast, undulating landscapes, there was a city named Jivaka, renowned for its thriving markets and illustrious scholars. But beyond the city's prosperous façade, many of its inhabitants grappled with a pressing dilemma. They were ensnared by the chains of materialism, constantly in pursuit of accumulating more wealth, always in competition, and perpetually dissatisfied. This race for riches rendered the streets of Jivaka paradoxically vibrant yet hollow.

Among the city's elite was a young noble named Arjun. His wealth was immeasurable, his estates vast, and his vaults overflowed with gold and precious gems. But his heart? It was an echoing cavern of emptiness and unquenched thirst.

One moonlit night, tormented by an overwhelming sense of unfulfillment, Arjun decided to leave his opulent mansion and venture into the wilderness in search of answers. His journey led him to the Himalayan foothills, where he encountered an old monk named Sariputra, meditating in a real cavern that resonated with a peculiar, haunting echo.

Arjun approached the monk and poured out his heart, expressing his wealth-induced desolation. Sariputra, having listened patiently, gestured to the echoing cavern around them.

"Do you hear the echo in this cavern, Arjun?" he asked.

Arjun nodded, "Yes, every sound seems to reverberate endlessly."

Sariputra continued, "Much like this cavern, your heart, despite being filled with wealth, echoes with emptiness because it seeks fulfillment in the material. Every coin you add only amplifies the echo of hollowness."

Dumbfounded, Arjun pondered upon the words. "But how do I quieten this echo, wise one?"

Sariputra smiled, "Seek richness not in gold but in experiences and deeds. Use your wealth not as an endpoint but as a means to enrich the world around you. Support the needy, promote education, and invest in creating opportunities for others. When your wealth becomes a bridge for others' aspirations, the echoing emptiness will be replaced by harmonious melodies of fulfillment."

Feeling enlightened, Arjun returned to Jivaka. He channeled his wealth towards building schools, hospitals, and public gardens. He supported artists, sponsored students, and opened up his estates for the homeless. Over time, the transformation wasn't just evident not only in Arjun but also in the fabric of Jivaka itself. The once hollow streets now resonated with laughter, gratitude, and tales of compassion.

Conclusion:
The story of Arjun and the echoing caverns sheds light on a profound truth of existence. True richness isn't about how much we possess but how we utilize what we have to impact the world positively. Wealth can become an instrument of profound change when seen as a means rather than an end. With its relentless emphasis on accumulation, the modern world often forgets this nuanced perspective. The challenge, then, is to redirect our pursuits to quieten the echoes of emptiness by fostering a world where wealth amplifies purpose, compassion, and collective progress.

THE LABYRINTH OF DESIRES

In the enchanting realm of Dharni, every individual at the age of twenty would enter the Labyrinth of Desires. This was no ordinary maze, for its winding paths and intricate turns were constructed not of stone or wood but of one's deepest yearnings and most unchecked aspirations. The promise was simple: navigate through the labyrinth successfully, and the heart's deepest materialistic desire would manifest in reality.

Vasana, a young woman of unparalleled intellect and spirit, was on the eve of her twentieth birthday. Her peers whispered eagerly about the luxury and opulence they hoped to gain from the labyrinth, from palatial mansions to chests filled with gleaming jewels. But Vasana, having seen many emerge from the maze with hallowed eyes and heavy hearts, held her reservations.

As she stepped into the labyrinth, the walls pulsated with visions of grandeur. Images of vast estates adorned with gold flashed before her eyes. Scenes of her being celebrated and revered, wearing the finest silks, and dining with kings and sages played out. The allure was undeniable. Each turn she took seemed to promise even more tantalizing prospects, and soon, Vasana found herself deeply ensnared, the exit nowhere in sight.

Days turned into weeks. The illusionary promises of the labyrinth now consumed the once clear-minded Vasana. The weight of her desires began to suffocate her, and hopelessness set in.

Then, in the labyrinth's darkest depths, Vasana encountered an old figure, her grandmother, Naropa, who had passed away years prior. Naropa, with eyes as deep and still as an ancient lake, beckoned Vasana closer.

"Lost in your desires, child?" she whispered.

Vasana, tears streaming down, nodded. "How do I find a way out, grandmother?"

Naropa held Vasana's face gently and said, "The labyrinth feeds on your materialistic wants, making them appear as needs. But true freedom and fulfillment lie not in possessing but in understanding, giving, and being."

Closing her eyes, Vasana took a deep breath. She started to let go of each materialistic desire, envisioning herself content without the luxury, without the adulation, focusing on love, compassion, and purpose. The walls of the labyrinth began to waver, the illusions fading.

As she took her final steps out, the world outside was not as she remembered. It was simpler but radiated a warmth and authenticity she had never perceived before. Vasana realized she hadn't just escaped a maze but transcended a mindset.

Conclusion:

The Labyrinth of Desires serves as a poignant allegory of our contemporary struggles. In a world driven by relentless consumerism and the race for more, we often find ourselves trapped in our own maze of escalating wants, mistaking them for needs. But true enlightenment and joy stem from realizing that life's essence isn't in the abundance of possessions but in the richness of our experiences, relationships, and personal growth. Breaking free requires not just recognizing this truth but internalizing and living it. It's a challenging perspective shift that promises a journey of genuine contentment and profound meaning.

THE ENIGMA OF SHATTERED MIRRORS

In the ethereal land of Alokik, a unique tradition was observed. Upon reaching the age of thirty, every individual was gifted a Mirror of Truth. This wasn't a mere reflective surface. The mirror possessed the power to reveal not one's physical appearance but the nature of one's soul, the depth of character, and the alignment of intentions.

Jayan, a compassionate healer known throughout Alokik for his selfless service, was eager as his thirtieth birthday approached. He had often heard tales of the Mirror of Truth and was curious about what insights his own soul might offer. He felt prepared, having dedicated his life to the well-being of others.

Jayan was handed his mirror on the designated day in a quiet, sacred chamber. Yet, as he gazed into it, no profound revelations met his eyes. Instead, the mirror simply shattered, fragments falling to the ground, leaving Jayan perplexed and the onlookers in hushed whispers.

Doubt clouded Jayan's mind. Had he misjudged his life's actions? Was there an unseen darkness within him that caused the mirror to shatter?

Desperate for answers, Jayan left Alokik, journeying through deserts, mountains, and vast plains in search of enlightenment. His travels brought him to a remote monastery perched high atop the Himalayas, where lived a sage known to possess the wisdom of the ages.

After listening to Jayan's tale, the sage, eyes twinkling with a hint of amusement, said, "Jayan, do you believe that a single mirror, even if termed as truth, holds the power to define your soul's worth?"

Jayan hesitated, "I thought it would provide clarity."

The sage responded, "Life isn't about seeking validation, even from mystical artifacts. The mirror shattered not because of any darkness within you but because your essence cannot be confined or defined by a singular perspective."

"But I've seen others gaze upon their mirrors, revealing beautiful, intricate patterns," Jayan protested.

The sage smiled, "Every soul has its own journey. Some find validation in patterns, while others, like you, are meant to transcend them. Your life's actions, your service to others, your love and compassion, they're immeasurable. They don't need a mirror's affirmation."

Reinvigorated, Jayan returned to Alokik, not with a reconstructed mirror but with a heart full of renewed purpose. He realized that seeking external validation, even from the mystical, can be limiting. True understanding comes from within, from recognizing one's unique path and embracing it wholeheartedly.

Conclusion:
The tale of Jayan and the shattered mirror challenges a prevalent mindset in our modern era, one of constant comparison and the quest for validation. In a world of curated perfection, where external validations often determine worth, it becomes essential to remember that true worth is intrinsic and immeasurable. Life isn't about fitting into pre-defined patterns but about forging our own unique path, irrespective of societal mirrors. Embracing this perspective isn't easy, but it's a liberating shift towards authenticity and genuine self-worth.

THE GARDEN OF FLEETING SHADOWS

In the harmonious realm of Prakriti, there was a renowned Garden of Fleeting Shadows. Its allure wasn't rooted in its flora or sparkling streams but in a peculiar phenomenon. Every tree in this garden cast a shadow, not of its own, but of one's most cherished material possession.

A merchant named Dhanan, known for his opulent lifestyle and insatiable appetite for riches, had heard tales of this garden but had never visited. Intrigued by the idea of seeing the shadow of his greatest treasure, he decided to make the journey.

Upon entering the garden, Dhanan eagerly approached a tall, majestic tree. He anticipated the shadow of his grandest mansion or perhaps his most prized jewel. Instead, to his dismay, he saw the faint shadow of a simple clay pot, a relic from his childhood, a symbol of a time when life was uncomplicated and joy was found in the smallest of things.

Disturbed and in disbelief, Dhanan approached another tree, then another, and another. Each time, the shadow remained unchanged – the modest clay pot.

Seeking answers, Dhanan approached the guardian of the garden, Maitri, and poured out his heart, questioning the veracity of the shadows. With a serene smile, Maitri responded, "This garden doesn't show the shadow of what you materially own but what truly owns a part of your soul. The clay pot is a reflection of your truest, most genuine self, unburdened by the weight of materialism."

Dhanan retorted, "But I've long moved past those days. I own treasures beyond measure now!"

Maitri gently said, "Material possessions are transient, no matter how grand. They come and go, but the essence of who you are, what truly resonates with your soul, remains constant. Perhaps the pot symbolizes the simplicity and authenticity you've left behind."

Dhanan spent days in the garden, reflecting upon Maitri's words. He realized that in his pursuit of material gains, he had lost touch with the pure, unadulterated joys of life. The clay pot, a humble object, represented genuine happiness, unattached to any price tag.

With newfound wisdom, Dhanan returned to his city. While he didn't abandon his riches, he reshaped his life, intertwining simplicity with opulence. He dedicated parts of his wealth to philanthropy, rediscovered lost passions, and rekindled relationships that had been sidelined in his pursuit of wealth.

Conclusion:

Dhanan's journey in the Garden of Fleeting Shadows offers a profound reflection on our modern society, which often measures success and happiness through material accomplishments. While wealth and possessions have their place, they shouldn't overshadow the intrinsic values and simple joys that truly enrich our lives. Recognizing and cherishing what genuinely resonates with our soul can lead to a more balanced, fulfilling existence. In a world driven by materialistic benchmarks, it's revolutionary to realize that sometimes, the most valuable treasures are the intangible memories, experiences, and emotions we hold dear.

THE MAZE OF TEMPTATION

In the heart of the Samanvaya Forest stood a labyrinth, famed not for its towering walls or complex pathways but for its unique essence. Unlike regular mazes, its walls were constructed of delicate, silken threads, each representing human desires.

A young, ambitious scholar named Vihara, who had read all scriptures and won many debates, sought to navigate this maze, confident he would find enlightenment at its center. He believed that with his vast knowledge and willpower, he could traverse the maze without getting ensnared.

As Vihara entered, he was immediately surrounded by threads so fine yet so strong. Each thread whispered promises of wealth, fame, power, and love. Feeling a tug, Vihara realized a particular thread had trapped him. It embodied his latent desire for unparalleled recognition. He struggled to break free, using his logical reasoning, only to get further entangled.

Hours turned into days. With each step, Vihara found himself wrapped in more threads, each representing deeper, subtler desires he hadn't recognized within himself. His knowledge seemed useless within these silken confines. Desperation crept in, and hope dwindled.

On the verge of giving up, an epiphany struck Vihara. He closed his eyes, focusing not on the threads but on the spaces between them. Instead of pushing against the threads, he gently navigated through the narrow gaps, moving with mindfulness and acceptance of his own vulnerabilities.

As days passed, Vihara's approach began yielding results. By embracing and understanding his desires rather than suppressing or combating them, he found a harmonious path through. The once intimidating maze felt less threatening, and the silken threads, though present, no longer held dominion over him.

Finally, at the labyrinth's heart, Vihara didn't find a treasure or a grand revelation but a serene pond, its waters reflecting his own image. It was a mirror to his transformed self, a testament to his journey from denial to acceptance.

Conclusion:

Vihara's odyssey is emblematic of our internal battles with desires. In a world that frequently tempts us with materialistic allurements, it's easy to become entangled, believing that suppression or sheer willpower is the way out. However, true liberation lies in understanding and accepting these desires, moving through life with awareness and balance. It's not the absence of desires but our relationship with them that determines our inner peace. Like Vihara, we too can navigate life's intricate maze, not by combating our nature but by harmonizing with it, understanding that the true essence of enlightenment often lies within the journey, not just the destination.

THE UNYIELDING TREE AND THE WHISPERING BREEZE

In the heart of the lush valley of Polonnaruwa, all beings lived in a harmonious dance with nature, save for one majestic tree named Bodhi. Bodhi stood firm, towering, and proud, its roots running deep and branches reaching out towards the heavens. Unlike the other trees, it prided itself on its unyielding nature, never swaying, no matter how strong the winds.

Across the valley, there was a gentle breeze named Milarepa. Unlike the tempestuous winds that roared through Polonnaruwa from time to time, Milarepa was soft-spoken, always whispering secrets of the universe to those who would listen.

One day, filled with playful curiosity, Milarepa approached the mighty Bodhi, hoping to share its whispers of wisdom.

But no matter how much Milarepa tried, Bodhi remained unmoved, proud of its resilience.

"You may have swayed others with your gentle words," boasted Bodhi, "but I am unyielding and unchanging."

Milarepa, unperturbed, whispered back, "Change is the essence of life, dear Bodhi. It's not about yielding but understanding. My whispers are not to challenge your strength but to share the beauty of impermanence."

Days turned into months, and Milarepa consistently returned to Bodhi, sharing tales of transformation, the rise and fall of mighty mountains, the ebb and flow of vast oceans, and the transient nature of life itself.

One evening, as the sun painted the sky in hues of gold and crimson, Milarepa whispered a story not of the world but of Bodhi's ancestors – seeds that transformed into saplings, young trees that weathered storms, and ancient trunks that once stood tall, only to return to the earth, nourishing countless generations.

The tale touched a chord deep within Bodhi, reminding it of its own journey from a fragile seed to the mighty tree it had become. For the first time, the unyielding tree swayed, not due to the force of the wind but the weight of realization.

Conclusion:

Bodhi's revelation in the company of Milarepa speaks to the very core of human nature. Often, in our quest for stability and permanence, we become rigid, resisting the natural flow of life. The wisdom lies not in resisting change but in understanding and embracing it. Impermanence, as whispered by Milarepa, is not a sign of weakness but the very essence of existence. In recognizing and appreciating the transient nature of life, one finds true strength and inner peace. It's through understanding the ever-changing dance of life that we come closer to the eternal truths of existence.

THE MIRROR LAKE OF SATI

In the serene lands of Majjhima, nestled between rolling hills and dense forests, there was a crystalline lake named Sati. Travelers from distant realms spoke of its unique quality: the lake mirrored not one's physical reflection but the deepest desires and sorrows of the soul.

Having heard tales of Sati's mysterious properties, an ascetic named Aruna embarked on a pilgrimage to the lake. As someone who had renounced all worldly desires, he was confident he'd see a calm and undisturbed reflection.

However, upon reaching the shores of Sati and gazing into its depths, Aruna was taken aback. Instead of the tranquility he expected, he saw visions of his past: memories of lost loved ones, missed opportunities, and deep-seated regrets. The lake stirred emotions he thought he had overcome.

Distraught, Aruna retreated to a nearby cave to meditate, seeking understanding. For seven days and nights, he sat in contemplation, diving deep into the recesses of his mind.

On the eighth morning, an elderly sage named Sujato appeared at the cave's entrance. Sensing Aruna's distress, the sage shared a parable.

"Imagine a lotus in the mud," Sujato began. "It rises above the murky waters, seeking the sun, untouched by the mire below. Yet, it is the very mud that nourishes it, allowing it to bloom."

Aruna pondered the words, seeking their deeper meaning.

Sujato continued, "Just like the lotus, our soul grows and evolves, nourished not just by joys but also by sorrows. Your reflection in Sati is not a sign of failure but a testament to your journey. The lake doesn't reveal these memories to cause pain but to illuminate the path of understanding and compassion."

As dawn broke, Aruna revisited Sati. This time, he didn't resist the memories but embraced them, realizing that each sorrow and joy had shaped him, guiding him on his spiritual path.

Conclusion:

Aruna's encounter with the Mirror Lake of Sati serves as a poignant reminder of the intricate tapestry of life woven with threads of joy, sorrow, love, and loss. Instead of shunning or denying these experiences, true understanding comes from acknowledging and embracing them. One finds the seeds of enlightenment and growth in the depths of Sati, or suffering. By facing and understanding our sorrows, we pave the way for deeper compassion, wisdom, and, ultimately, liberation.

THE GOLDEN CAGE OF SUNYATA

In the vibrant city of Upekkha, there stood a grand bazaar known to all as the marketplace of desires. One of its countless stalls was particularly eye-catching, displaying a magnificent golden cage. Its bars were intricately carved with symbols of power, wealth, and fame.

A hermit named Loka, renowned for his wisdom and detachment, wandered into the bazaar. Curious onlookers wondered what such a sage might seek in a place of worldly desires. Approaching the golden cage, Loka inquired about the price.

The merchant, recognizing the hermit, chuckled, "For you, revered one, the cage is not for sale. But, if you wish, you may look inside."

Peering through the bars, Loka saw not a bird but a miniature version of himself, looking distressed and trapped. The sight was unsettling.

Seeing Loka's reaction, the merchant explained, "This cage, sage, represents the traps of worldly desires. The mini-you inside is trapped by the allure of gold, power, and fame. Many see this and recognize their own bondage, yet they still yearn for the cage, hoping to possess it, mistakenly believing it's the cage they desire, not realizing it's freedom they truly seek."

Loka, with a glint in his eye, whispered a prayer. As his chant resonated, the mini-him inside the cage started to fade, and the cage's golden bars turned to dust, revealing a lotus in bloom where the cage once stood.

The crowd gasped in amazement. Addressing the gathering, Loka shared, "The cage is an illusion, a construct of our desires. True wealth isn't possessing the golden cage but realizing the Sunyata, the emptiness of such desires. In this understanding, one is set free, much like the blooming lotus, unbound by the mud beneath."

Conclusion:
Loka's profound interaction with the golden cage imparts an age-old wisdom – the ephemeral nature of materialistic desires. While the allure of wealth, fame, and power is undeniable, it's often these very desires that cage our spirit, preventing true growth and understanding. It's not about renouncing the world but understanding its transient nature. By doing so, like Loka, we can rise above the illusory cages that bind us, blooming in the fullness of our spiritual journey.

THE SILKEN THREAD OF SAMADHI

Deep in the serene valley of Vipassana, villagers often spoke of an ancient and mystic loom, said to weave fabrics unseen and untouched by ordinary beings. This loom, named Samadhi, was no ordinary contraption. Instead of threads, it wove with intangible strands of human emotions, experiences, and thoughts.

A young seeker named Vira, thirsty for enlightenment, heard tales of the loom and embarked on a journey to find it. Guided by whispers of old trees and songs of meandering rivers, she finally reached the cave where Samadhi was said to reside.

Inside the dimly lit cave, Vira found the loom. To her surprise, it wasn't working. Instead of the rhythmic sound of weaving, there was a stark silence. Upon closer inspection, she noticed a single silken thread, shimmering with a golden hue, just out of the loom's grasp.

Determined, Vira tried to place the thread onto the loom. But each time she tried, the thread would slip through her fingers, eluding capture. Hours turned to days, and yet the thread remained untamed.

On the third day, an elderly monk named Karuna visited the cave. Observing Vira's struggle, he gently whispered, "The thread you try to grasp is not outside but within."

Confused, Vira replied, "But master, it's right here, shimmering and real."

With a gentle smile, Karuna responded, "That thread represents Samadhi, a state of deep meditative consciousness. It isn't something to be forcefully woven or captured. Instead, it's an inner journey, realized through surrender and understanding."

Taking the cue, Vira closed her eyes, took deep breaths, and delved within. She meditated, letting go of her desires and expectations. As her inner tumult calmed, she felt a profound connection, a union with the universe. When she opened her eyes, the loom was weaving harmoniously, the golden thread seamlessly integrating, crafting a fabric that radiated serenity.

Conclusion:
The story of Vira and the loom, Samadhi, serves as a reminder of the intricate dance between effort and surrender in our spiritual journey. The pursuit of Samadhi isn't about external conquests but internal realization. The silken thread, seemingly elusive, becomes

accessible when one ceases to chase and starts to introspect. In embracing the inner journey with genuine curiosity and humility, one can weave the fabric of enlightenment, interlaced with threads of understanding, compassion, and unity.

THE CURRENCY OF STILLNESS

In the bustling metropolis of Dhammapada, people thrived on commerce and innovation. The heartbeat of the city was its central square, where traders, scholars, and artisans converged, making it a hub of activity. In this square stood a grand bank, known not for gold or jewels but for a unique currency: moments of stillness.

Every resident, from the wealthiest merchant to the humblest laborer, would queue up to deposit their moments of quiet introspection. These weren't physical coins or notes but memories of genuine silence and reflection. The richer the experience, the more valuable the deposit.

A young entrepreneur named Anicca, obsessed with success, had never set foot in this bank. To her, time was money, and every moment was an opportunity for growth. Stillness, she believed, was a luxury she couldn't afford.

One evening, as Anicca hurriedly walked past the bank, she found herself inexplicably drawn to its grand entrance. She stepped inside to see a world quite unlike any she had known. Instead of the clamor of commerce, there was a profound silence. At the counters, patrons stood with eyes closed, immersing themselves in deep contemplation.

Curiosity piqued, Anicca approached a teller and asked, "What is the value of this stillness? How does it benefit?"

The teller, an old woman with eyes that sparkled with wisdom, replied, "Dear child, in stillness, one finds clarity. With clarity comes understanding. And with understanding, the true wealth of life is revealed."

Challenged by this perspective, Anicca decided to make a deposit. Finding a quiet corner, she closed her eyes, pushing away thoughts of business and ambition. Minutes turned to hours, and when she emerged from her meditation, she felt a tranquility she had never known.

Over time, Anicca became the bank's most regular patron. She realized that the moments of stillness didn't detract from her success; they enhanced it. With clarity of thought, her decisions became more astute, her interactions more genuine, and her life more fulfilled.

Conclusion:

In the rapid pace of modern life, we often undervalue the currency of stillness, mistaking activity for achievement. Anicca's journey in Dhammapada reminds us that in moments of quiet reflection, we discover our deepest insights and our truest selves. By honoring stillness, we don't lose time; we gain perspective. And in that perspective lies the true wealth of existence, far more valuable than any material possession.

THE RESONANCE OF TRUE DESIRES

The picturesque town of Vimuktin sat nestled between mountains, renowned for its pristine lake, which had a peculiar well at its heart. This well, named Tanha, was no ordinary one; it was said to echo the deepest desires of anyone who peered into it.

An ambitious young writer named Maya, seeking inspiration for her next story, traveled to Vimuktin upon hearing about Tanha. She stood by the well, gazing into its depths, waiting to hear the echo of her heart's true desire.

To her surprise, a cacophony of voices reverberated instead of a single echo, each voicing distinct ambitions — fame, love, wealth, recognition. Maya felt overwhelmed, realizing that these were all her desires, each clamoring for attention.

Distressed, Maya approached an old sage named Nirvana, who lived nearby. Pouring out her heart, she said, "I thought

I knew what I wanted, but the well shows me a storm of desires. How do I find my true calling?"

After a moment of contemplation, Nirvana responded, "The well merely mirrors the tumult within most human hearts. To hear your truest desire, you must first quieten the noise."

Taking his words to heart, Maya sat by the lake, meditating, focusing on her breath, and gently acknowledging each desire without judgment. Days turned into weeks. As the layers of fleeting wants dissolved, a profound, pure, and singular desire resonated from the well – the yearning to connect deeply with others through her words.

With newfound clarity, Maya wrote her masterpiece not for fame or fortune but from the genuine wish to touch souls. The story became a beacon of hope and understanding for many, reflecting their own struggles and aspirations.

Conclusion:

In the relentless chase of life, we often accumulate desires, mistaking quantity for quality. The well of Tanha mirrors our inner turmoil, reflecting the myriad wants that frequently drown our truest callings. Maya's journey teaches us that by peeling back the layers of superficial longings and delving into introspection, we can discern the core desires that truly resonate with our essence. Such desires, pursued with sincerity, lead not just to personal fulfillment but also to profound connections with the world around us.

THE UNSEEN GARDEN OF DUKKHA

In the secluded valleys of Theravada, where the lotus blooms touched the sky, and the rivers whispered ancient tales, lay a walled garden named Dukkha. It was said that this garden bore fruits of unparalleled taste but was also entwined with thorns of profound pain. Few dared to venture in, and fewer came out unchanged.

One day, a scholar named Metta, intrigued by tales of the garden, decided to explore it. The townspeople warned him, "The pleasures of Dukkha are ephemeral, but the scars last a lifetime." Undeterred, Metta, armed with his wisdom and texts, stepped into the garden.

As he ventured deeper, the alluring aroma of fruits intoxicated him. He tasted them and found moments of sheer bliss but was soon pricked by the concealed thorns, each representing life's various sufferings – loss, jealousy, greed, and more. A memory of pain surfaced with every prick, and the fruit's sweetness turned bitter.

Overwhelmed by the duality of joy and pain, Metta sought refuge under the Bodhi tree at the garden's heart. There, he met an aged monk named Panna, known to be the voice of Buddhaghosa.

Seeking guidance, Metta asked, "Why does such sweetness carry such pain?"

With a serene smile, Panna responded, "Just as the lotus blooms in mud, life's joys are intertwined with sufferings. But look deeper, young scholar. Beyond the duality lies the middle path, leading to liberation."

Guided by Panna, Metta meditated, detaching from the allure of the fruits and the fear of thorns. He observed his desires, pains, and pleasures without attachment. Days turned into nights, seasons changed, and a profound realization dawned upon him: it was not the garden that bound him but his reactions to it.

Emerging from his meditation, Metta saw Dukkha not as a maze of pleasure and pain but as a reflection of life itself. He understood that liberation lay not in avoiding suffering but in understanding and transcending it.

Grateful, Metta approached Panna, "The garden hasn't changed, but I see it with new eyes."

Panna nodded, "Dukkha remains, but your bondage to it has dissolved. You now walk the middle path."

Conclusion:

The Garden of Dukkha stands as a metaphor for life, brimming with joys and challenges. Metta's journey reflects our own struggles, swinging between pleasure and pain, often lost in life's labyrinth. But, as Panna's wisdom unveils, the key to navigating this maze isn't in the external world but within. By understanding and transcending our attachments and aversions, we can find the middle path, leading to a deeper understanding, acceptance, and, eventually, liberation.

THE SILVER COIN'S JOURNEY

In a bustling town named Kalpana, the marketplace was the heart of all activity. Traders, artisans, and common folk all assembled there, exchanging goods, stories, and laughter. At the center of this marketplace was a modest shop owned by Arun, a kind-hearted merchant.

One day, a monk named Nagarjuna visited Arun's shop. Having just sold a cherished artifact, Nagarjuna had a single, shiny silver coin. He handed the coin to Arun in exchange for a simple robe. As their hands met, Nagarjuna whispered, "This coin, Arun, is not just metal. It's a lesson waiting to be learned."

Curious, Arun watched as the coin journeyed through Kalpana. It first went to Piyadassi, a baker, who gave it to Lata, a flower seller, for her fragrant blossoms. Lata then used it to buy a toy for her child from a toymaker named Dev.

As days turned to weeks, the coin moved from hand to hand, never resting. Arun noticed something intriguing. Upon receiving the coin, each holder felt a momentary surge of joy, anticipating what it could bring. Yet, once it left their hands, a fleeting sense of loss followed, only to be replaced by desire once more.

Months passed, and the coin found its way back to Arun, offered by a young boy in exchange for a loaf of bread. Holding the coin again, Arun pondered on its journey and the myriad emotions it evoked. The coin itself hadn't changed, but it held a mirror to the human dance of desire and detachment.

Seeking understanding, Arun visited Nagarjuna, who was now meditating in a grove outside Kalpana. "This coin," Arun began, "it brings both joy and sorrow. Is it a blessing or a curse?"

Nagarjuna smiled, "It's neither. It's a teacher. The coin doesn't carry joy or sorrow; it merely reveals the nature of our attachments. The joy of possession, the pain of parting, all lie within us, not in the coin."

Conclusion:

Our lives, like the marketplace of Kalpana, are filled with exchanges. We chase desires, clutching and letting go, often attributing our happiness or sorrow to external objects or events. Yet, like the silver coin, these externalities are merely mirrors reflecting our internal states. True contentment arises not from possession but from understanding the nature of our desires and the impermanence of all things. Embracing this wisdom, we can navigate the marketplace of life with grace, equanimity, and profound joy.

THE SYMPHONY OF SILHOUETTES

In the ancient city of Rajgir, where shadows whispered, and winds carried the scent of forgotten times, lived souls painted in various hues of life, each silhouette representing different facets of existence. However, these shadows were bound by invisible strings to the Silhouette Tree, a divine entity in the city center.

Amongst the citizens was a sculptor named Sumedho, known for his creations breathing life and emotion. However, he longed to sculpt the invisible strings that bound the shadows, to give form to the formless connections between beings.

In pursuit of his quest, Sumedho approached the venerable sage, Santi, who was said to be the echo of the divine voice. "O wise one," Sumedho implored, "how can I give form to the unseen bonds that intertwine our destinies?"

His eyes reflect the cosmos, and Santi replies, "The unseen is the symphony of existence, the rhythm of the cosmos. To see it, you must listen to the silence, feel the void, and embrace the essence of being."

With Santi's words echoing in his soul, Sumedho began his inward journey, sitting beneath the Silhouette Tree, opening his senses to the unseen symphony. Days melded into nights, the moon danced with the sun, and slowly, the silent symphony began to reveal itself.

Sumedho sensed the delicate vibrations, the cosmic dance of interbeing in the profound silence. He felt the subtle strings connecting all existence, the harmonious symphony of the universe unfolding in every moment.

With newfound insight, Sumedho sculpted not with his hands but with his soul, giving form to the formless and shape to the shapeless. His creation depicted the invisible symphony, the interconnected dance of all beings, each shadow interwoven with another, creating a harmonious tapestry of existence.

His masterpiece, "The Symphony of Silhouettes," became a beacon for souls seeking the unseen, a gateway to experiencing the interconnected dance of life. People from distant lands came to witness the silent symphony, to lose and find themselves in the intricate dance of shadows.

Conclusion:

Sumedho's pursuit and eventual revelation symbolize our intrinsic yearning to understand the unperceived connections of existence, the invisible strings that bind us all. The essence of the unseen lies not in the visible realm but in the silent symphony of the cosmos, where every being is a note, forming the harmonious melody of existence. By delving into our inner silence and embracing the essence of being, we can perceive the interconnected dance of life and realize that in the grand tapestry of existence, we are not isolated threads but integral parts of the whole. The realization of this harmonious interconnection is a step towards a profound transformation, allowing us to perceive and embrace existence in its entirety.

THE TAPESTRY OF DREAMS

In the verdant valley of Siddhim, nestled between mountains that seemed to touch the heavens, was a village where dreams were weaved into reality. The villagers were known far and wide as the Dreamweavers.

Every household in Siddhim had a loom, and from young to old, everyone contributed threads to the grand tapestry of life. It was said that the colors of their tapestries were sourced not from dyes but from the emotions and experiences of the weaver.

Young Tara, curious and bright-eyed, was learning the art from her grandmother, Mira. Each day, Mira would narrate tales of her youth, and with every story, Tara noticed a distinct shade emerging on the loom.

One evening, after a particularly heartfelt tale of lost love, Tara asked, "Grandma, why is it that stories of pain weave such beautiful patterns? Why do not the happy tales shine as bright?"

While pausing her work, Mira looked deep into Tara's eyes and said, "My child, happiness is like the clear blue sky, vast and serene. But it is the clouds of sorrow, the storms of trials, and the rain of tears that bring depth to that expanse. Just as a cloudless sky might seem empty, a life without challenges lacks depth."

Tara contemplated her grandmother's words. The next day, she began weaving her own experiences into the tapestry. The days of laughter, the nights of tears, the moments of doubt, and the times of revelation. As her fingers moved, she noticed the tapestry wasn't just a reflection of her life but also a guide, showing her the interconnectedness of joy and sorrow, success and failure.

Years passed, and Tara became the village's most celebrated Dreamweaver. Travelers from distant lands came to witness her tapestries, which seemed alive with emotion.

One day, a young woman, eyes filled with tears, stood before one of Tara's tapestries. "It's like you've woven my heart into this," she whispered.

Tara approached her, "Our lives might be different, but our emotions, experiences, and lessons are interwoven. Through this tapestry, I merely remind you of your own strength and the beauty of your journey."

Conclusion:

Life, in all its unpredictability, presents us with a spectrum of experiences. Often, we categorize them as 'good' or 'bad,' seeking endless joys and avoiding sorrows. But just as the tapestry gains its beauty from diverse threads, our lives find depth and meaning through varied experiences. By embracing every emotion, every challenge, and every joy, we not only enrich our lives but also weave tales that resonate across hearts, reminding each other of our shared journey and the profound beauty within it.

Karma and the Law of Cause and Effect

In the course of our lives, the principle of karma plays a profound role in shaping our experiences and destinies. The tales in this book vividly illustrate the interconnectedness of actions and their consequences, reflecting the philosophies of Buddhism, Taoism, and Ikigai. By understanding karma, we are invited to live with greater mindfulness and intention, recognizing that our actions today shape our future.

The Essence of Karma

Karma, derived from the Sanskrit word for "action," is not about fate or predetermined destiny but about the intentional acts that shape our lives. These actions can be positive, negative, or neutral, depending on the motivations behind them. Positive actions stem from compassion, generosity, and wisdom, leading to beneficial outcomes. Negative actions arise from greed, hatred, and ignorance, resulting in suffering. Neutral actions, although having no immediate karmic consequences, can still influence future experiences based on their underlying intentions.

Buddhism: The Web of Karma

In Buddhism, karma is a central doctrine that underscores the law of cause and effect. This principle states that every action—whether physical, verbal, or mental—creates an imprint on our consciousness, shaping our present and future experiences. Understanding karma is pivotal for personal growth and ethical living, as it guides individuals to act with intention and mindfulness.

It teaches that karma is the law of moral causation, where every action has a corresponding reaction. Good actions lead to positive outcomes, while negative actions result in suffering. This principle underscores the importance of ethical conduct and mindfulness in every aspect of life.

One of the key teachings of karma is the importance of taking responsibility for our actions. Buddhism teaches that we are the creators of our own karma and that we have the power to shape our destiny through our thoughts, words, and deeds. By cultivating positive qualities such as compassion and wisdom, we can create a more peaceful and harmonious world. This understanding encourages us to live ethically, knowing that our actions have far-reaching consequences.

In the stories within this chapter, characters often face the repercussions of their actions, embodying the Buddhist understanding of karma. For instance, "The Orchard of Choices" illustrates how decisions lead to corresponding outcomes, highlighting the moral causation that good actions bring positive results and negative actions lead to suffering. Similarly, "The Pottery of Fate" showcases a character who faces downfall due to deceitful actions, mirroring the Buddhist teaching that our actions are seeds that grow into the fruits of our future experiences.

Taoism: The Flow of Natural Consequences

Taoism, an ancient Chinese philosophy and religion, emphasizes living in harmony with the Tao (the Way). Unlike the more linear concept of karma found in Buddhism, Taoism focuses on the natural flow and balance of life, where every action has a corresponding reaction within the broader tapestry of the universe. Understanding Taoist principles of cause and effect can profoundly change our perception of life's events and guide us towards a harmonious and fulfilling existence.

The Flow of the Tao

In Taoism, the universe operates through a natural order that is best understood through the concept of the Tao. The Tao is an all-encompassing force that underlies and unifies everything. The Tao Te Ching, a cornerstone of Taoist philosophy, teaches that living in accordance with this natural order leads to a balanced and peaceful life. This involves embracing simplicity, humility, and spontaneity, allowing life to unfold without unnecessary interference.

Wu Wei: Action Without Effort

A central tenet of Taoism is *wu wei*, often translated as "non-action" or "effortless action." This principle advises acting in accordance with the natural flow of events rather than striving against them. *Wu wei* does not imply inaction but encourages actions that are in harmony with the Tao. When we act without attachment to outcomes, we align ourselves with the natural order, reducing friction and promoting harmony.

In the story "The Unseen Balance," characters learn to find peace by aligning their actions with the natural order. This reflects the Taoist belief that true balance and harmony come from living in accordance with the Tao.

Yin and Yang: The Balance of Opposites

Taoism emphasizes the concept of yin and yang, representing the dualistic nature of reality where opposites coexist and complement each other. This balance is crucial in understanding cause and effect within Taoist philosophy. Every action and its effect are seen as part of a dynamic balance. For example, good and bad, success and failure, are all necessary parts of the whole and contribute to the balance of life.

"The Dance of the Celestial Lotus" illustrates the importance of finding harmony through balance. Characters in the story achieve peace by understanding and embracing the dualities of life, such as effort and rest, action and stillness.

Taoist Perspective on Cause and Effect

While Taoism does not have a direct equivalent to the Buddhist concept of karma, it recognizes a form of cause and effect rooted in the natural order. Actions in alignment with the Tao lead to harmony, while actions against the Tao lead to discord. This understanding encourages a way of life that is mindful of the natural consequences of our actions, promoting a holistic and integrated approach to living.

In "The Pottery of Fate," characters discover that their actions, when aligned with the natural order, bring about harmony and success. Conversely, actions driven by greed and ego lead to imbalance and misfortune.

Living in Harmony with the Tao

Taoism teaches that by understanding and aligning with the Tao, we can live a life of greater ease and less resistance. This involves cultivating virtues such as humility, compassion, and simplicity. The tales in this chapter highlight how characters learn to live in harmony with the Tao, finding peace and fulfillment in the process.

For instance, "The Reflective Orchard of Padma" explores how a character finds joy and purpose by nurturing an orchard in alignment with the natural cycles. This story emphasizes that true fulfillment comes from actions that respect and harmonize with nature.

Ikigai: Purposeful Actions and Their Impact

The law of cause and effect, fundamental to many philosophies, asserts that every action has a corresponding reaction. In the context of Ikigai, this law highlights the importance of intentional actions and their impacts on our lives. By understanding this principle, we can make conscious choices that lead to positive outcomes and fulfillment.

The stories in this chapter highlight how discovering and living one's Ikigai leads to a fulfilling life, shaped by the positive impact of purposeful actions.

In "The Reflective Orchard of Padma," a character discovers their Ikigai through nurturing an orchard, finding joy and fulfillment in the act of creation and contribution to the community. This aligns with the Ikigai principle that purposeful actions lead to a fulfilling and impactful life. Similarly, "The River of Samsara" depicts a protagonist who finds his reason for being by helping others navigate life's challenges, demonstrating that living with purpose and intention brings profound satisfaction and positive ripples through the community.

THE ORCHARD OF CHOICES

In a tranquil village nestled between two verdant mountains, there lived a kind farmer named Pasanno. He owned an orchard filled with every kind of fruit imaginable. Residents and travelers alike often commented on the magnificent spectrum of colors his orchard presented. However, there was a peculiar thing about this orchard; half of it bore succulent, sweet fruits, while the other half produced sour, inedible ones.

One day, a traveler named Arya visited the village. Having heard tales of Pasanno's famed orchard, he was curious to understand the mystery behind the contrasting produce.

"Good Pasanno," Arya began, "Why is it that half of your orchard thrives with delicious fruits while the other half suffers?"

Pasanno smiled, hinting at a deeper understanding, beckoned Arya to walk with him. "Observe closely," Pasanno said, handing Arya a sweet fruit from the flourishing side.

Arya took a bite and was instantly enveloped by its delightful flavor. "This is the result of years of tender care, of ensuring that the soil is nurtured, and of singing lullabies to the trees during chilly nights."

They then moved to the other half of the orchard, and Pasanno handed Arya a fruit. Its bitterness was overwhelming. "This side," Pasanno began, "was once like the other. But I neglected it. I believed that once planted, the trees would fend for themselves. I gave them neither attention nor love."

Arya pondered this. "But surely, the trees, being of the same land, should bear similar fruits?"

Pasanno chuckled. "Much like the fruits, our actions, too, have outcomes. If we foster kindness, patience, and diligence, our lives reflect those virtues. However, if we act out of greed, anger, or ignorance, life becomes as bitter as the fruits from this side of my orchard. This is the law of Karma."

Upon reflection, Arya felt a weight lift off his shoulders. It was as if he understood a fundamental truth about life.

Conclusion:

In life, much like in Pasanno's orchard, our actions determine the outcomes we face. The law of Karma, or cause and effect, illustrates that our choices, whether driven by kindness or malice, will always circle back to us. Understanding this profound principle allows us to navigate our lives with greater consciousness, ensuring that the "fruits" we reap align with the seeds we sow. Just as Pasanno realized the importance of nurturing each tree, we must recognize the significance of every deed, every word, and every intention. The universe has an impeccable memory. Every cause has an effect, and every action has a consequence.

THE UNSEEN BALANCE

In a bustling city named Kunzang, overshadowed by gleaming skyscrapers and modern amenities, there sat an ancient temple that had withstood the passage of time. This temple was home to an unusual scale known to the city dwellers as the Scale of Tamas.

This was no ordinary scale. It had two trays: one, gleaming gold and always shining, no matter the hour; the other, a dark abyss, seemingly consuming all light around it. The peculiar thing about this scale was that it always remained balanced, never tilting one way or the other, despite appearing to be empty.

Anika, a spirited young journalist, was intrigued by this phenomenon. Why did this scale never tip? Why did it remain in the heart of such a modern city? With these questions swirling in her mind, she approached the temple's caretaker, an old monk named Varun.

"Venerable Varun," Anika began, "What secret does this scale hold? Why does it never tip?"

Varun, with wise eyes that seemed to have witnessed countless sunrises and sunsets, beckoned her closer. "Each tray," he whispered, "represents our actions. The gleaming tray stands for our positive deeds, the kindness and love we spread. The dark tray embodies our negative actions, the pain and hurt we might cause."

"But why is it always balanced?" Anika pressed.

Varun smiled, "Because the universe ensures a balance, dear child. Every action has a reaction. Every deed, good or bad, reverberates throughout the cosmos, affecting the balance of the scale. Even if we don't see it immediately, the universe keeps a tally."

"But how does that challenge our conventional understanding?" Anika inquired.

Varun responded, "Many believe that their deeds, especially the unnoticed ones, go without consequence. They believe that if no one sees, it doesn't matter. But this scale is a reminder that even in secret, every act counts. The universe always balances the scale."

Overwhelmed with realization, Anika saw the city and its dwellers in a new light. Every act of kindness, every harsh word, every hidden deed, was all part of a grander design.

Conclusion:
The Scale of Tamas serves as a poignant reminder that the universe, in its vast expanse, maintains a meticulous record of our actions. The principle of Karma isn't just about overt repercussions. It challenges our deeply-held belief that unnoticed deeds fade into oblivion. Instead, they echo in the universe, impacting the delicate balance of life. The unseen balance teaches us to tread thoughtfully, understanding that every action, seen or unseen, contributes to the cosmic dance of cause and effect.

THE POTTERY OF FATE

Amidst the vast desert expanse of Maru, there existed a single town named Vayu. This town had a unique characteristic: no secrets could be kept. Every whispered conversation was carried by the wind, eventually reaching every ear in Vayu.

Jaya, a talented potter of the town, was known for her unmatched skill and the beauty of her creations. However, she harbored jealousy towards another potter, Ravi, whose popularity was steadily rising. One day, giving in to her envy, she discreetly sabotaged Ravi's kiln, ensuring his pots would crack upon firing.

Believing her deed to be secret, she was startled when, the next morning, her own kiln malfunctioned, destroying her creations. Moreover, hushed conversations about her act danced in the wind, filling her ears wherever she went.

Distraught and ashamed, Jaya approached the town's wise elder, Nalini, seeking solace. "Why, Nalini, did the wind betray me? Why did my own kiln turn against me?"

Nalini, with the wisdom of ages evident in her gaze, replied, "The wind, dear Jaya, did not betray you. It merely echoed the universe's sentiment. In Maru, as in life, our actions and our karma reverberate back to us. What we send forth into the world has a way of finding its way back, be it good or ill."

Jaya pondered deeply upon this. "But in our world," she retorted, "many deeds, good and bad, seem to go unnoticed. Many misdeeds never meet their deserved fate."

Nalini responded with a serene smile, "Just because the echo isn't heard immediately doesn't mean it won't return. The universe's ledger is intricate, and time plays its part. One might not witness the echo of their deeds in the way they expect or in the timeframe they hope, but it invariably returns."

In time, Jaya mended her ways, and her pottery flourished. The whispers of the wind turned from reprimands to praises. Not only did she rebuild Ravi's kiln, but the two became collaborators, combining their skills to create unparalleled masterpieces.

Conclusion:

The tale of Vayu offers a profound reflection on the nature of karma and the intricate law of cause and effect. It challenges the prevalent notion that actions without immediate consequences are inconsequential. Instead, it prompts us to consider the broader canvas of time and the myriad ways the universe might echo our deeds. The wind's whispers remind us to act with consciousness, knowing that every deed, whether whispered or shouted, contributes to the symphony of our existence.

THE ENIGMA OF LUSHAN'S BRIDGE

Lushan, a remote village, was nestled deep in the cradle of a verdant valley. Its most prized possession was an ancient bridge, which, despite appearing frail and weather-worn, never broke, even under the heaviest load. Legend said it was the embodiment of Karma itself.

Wangmo, a city dweller, having heard tales of this bridge, visited Lushan. Her life in the city was marked by impatience, opportunism, and an undying pursuit of success at any cost. To her, the world was binary — cause and effect, action and reward. The tales of the bridge intrigued her; how could such a fragile structure withstand such weight?

Upon reaching the village, she was greeted by an old sage, Ming, the keeper of the bridge's legend. With her usual directness, Wangmo asked, "What makes this bridge so special? Why doesn't it break?"

Ming beckoned her to walk on the bridge. As she stepped on it, the wood beneath her feet vibrated with energy, and she saw fleeting images – moments from her past, decisions she made, people she'd wronged.

"The bridge," Ming began in a hushed tone, "reflects your Karma. It doesn't break from the physical weight but from the weight of one's deeds. It stands as a testament to the balance of life – it's not just our actions but the intentions behind them that weigh us down."

Dumbfounded, Wangmo realized that her success, achieved at the expense of others, was a weight she was carrying. "But I've been successful," she argued, "I've never felt this weight."

Looking deep into the horizon, Ming responded, "The Law of Cause and Effect isn't as straightforward as you deem. Often, we bear the weight internally – through restlessness, guilt, or an insatiable hunger for more. The universe has its rhythm, its ebb, and flow. What we give, we get back, maybe not today or tomorrow, but in moments unexpected."

Over the next days, Wangmo spent time in Lushan, learning from the villagers, understanding the beauty of balance and the silent yet profound way the universe echoes our deeds. Her worldview shifted from chasing success to seeking harmony.

Conclusion:

Lushan's Bridge serves as a symbolic reminder of the intricate and often unseen ways Karma weaves into our lives. It challenges the simplistic perspective of immediate retribution and urges one to see the broader, often invisible, tapestry of cause and effect. Every action, every intention, casts a stone in the vast river of existence, creating ripples that travel far and wide. The bridge implores us to tread with awareness, understanding that the weight of our choices is both immediate and echoing.

NIRAYA'S ENCHANTED GARDEN

Deep within the heartland of the region known as Niraya, there was a fabled garden named Niraya's Whisper. It was said that any seed sown in this garden would bear fruit in a single night. But there was a catch. The fruits yielded were never based on the seeds sown but rather on the intention of the planter.

Rohan, a wealthy merchant from a neighboring city, heard of this garden. Greed clouded his vision, and he imagined the wealth he could accumulate if he could harness the garden's power. He sought the finest, most exotic seeds, dreaming of the extraordinary fruits they'd bear.

One evening, he secretly entered the garden and planted his chosen seeds. Imagining a bounty of exotic fruits that he could sell for a fortune, he eagerly returned the following dawn. To his astonishment, he found not the envisioned exotic fruits but thorny bushes laden with bitter fruits.

Perplexed, he approached the village's elder, Yara. With wisdom etched into every wrinkle on her face, she explained, "This garden doesn't yield based on the seed, but rather on the intent. Your greed gave birth to these thorns."

Determined to harness the garden's power, Rohan tried again. This time, he planted ordinary seeds but with the intention of sharing any produce with the village. The following day, he was greeted with an abundance of the most delicious, exotic fruits he could have imagined.

Excited, he asked Yara, "Why is this garden so different? Why doesn't it follow the simple law of planting and harvesting?"

With a twinkle in her eyes, Yara replied, "Isn't life much like our garden? We often expect direct outcomes for our actions, but life – in its infinite wisdom – responds not just to our actions but to our intentions, our emotions, and the energy we release. It's a dance of cause and effect that transcends the physical realm."

Rohan was humbled. He realized the profound truth in the workings of Niraya's Whisper. He transformed his business, ensuring fairness, charity, and kindness were at its core.

Conclusion:

Niraya's Whisper isn't merely a tale of a magical garden. It's a reflection of life's intricate tapestry woven with the threads of karma. The story challenges the linear perception of cause and effect, urging us to recognize the profound depths of our intentions and their ripple effects in the universe. It's not just the act but the heart behind the act that shapes our destiny. In this realization lies the essence of a conscious, harmonious existence.

THE DANCE OF THE CELESTIAL LOTUS

In the harmonious cradle of the realm named Mettachandra, there blossomed a divine lotus, Dharmaraja, bathed in celestial light, whispering secrets of existence to those who would listen. Its petals were said to hold the tapestry of life's intricate dance of cause and effect, and each whisper was a symphony of cosmic truths.

There lived in Mettachandra a humble artisan, Karunakar, who crafted delicate fabrics, subtly whispering tales of wisdom. But within her tender heart, there lingered a silent thirst — a thirst to weave the cosmic dance of Dharmaraja into her fabrics.

One serene night, enveloped by the moon's silver glow, she approached the celestial lotus. With reverent steps and a heart full of longing, she whispered, "O Dharmaraja, let me weave your dance, the silent symphony of existence, into my fabrics."

The lotus, its celestial light shimmering, responded with a delicate whisper, "Karunakar, to weave my dance, you must understand the unseen rhythm of the universe, the echo of actions and intentions in the boundless dance of existence."

Karunakar, with a heart ablaze with divine yearning, absorbed the whispers of Dharmaraja. She meditated on the subtle rhythms of existence, observing the unseen strings connecting actions to their echoes, intentions to their reflections.

As her understanding deepened, her loom became a dance of cosmic harmony. She wove the unseen rhythms, the delicate balance of actions and their reflections, the silent symphony of intentions and their echoes.

Her fabrics became whispers of Dharmaraja, each thread a silent hymn of cosmic balance. Those who draped themselves in her creations felt the unseen dance of existence, the harmony of actions, and their celestial echoes.

Conclusion:

The Dance of the Celestial Lotus is not just a tale of divine yearning and cosmic harmony. It is a delicate reminder of the unseen, intricate dance of cause and effect in our existence. It invites the seeker to reflect on the profound interplay of actions and intentions, to observe the subtle, celestial echoes in the boundless symphony of existence. It's a whisper to perceive not just the seen but to embrace the unseen rhythms, to dance in harmony with the divine tapestry of life, understanding that every action, every intention, is a note in the celestial symphony of the cosmos.

THE GOLDEN SCALES OF JIVANA

In a realm cocooned between the layers of reality and dreams flowed the serene River Jivana. Its waters were crystal clear, yet they held a unique characteristic: they reflected not the physical form but the true essence of one's actions and intentions.

Beside the river sat a golden scale, ancient and untouched by time. Unlike ordinary scales, this one weighed not objects but the weight of one's karmic deeds.

Tsultrim, a curious wanderer from the nearby village of Anupama, had often heard of these magical scales but had never ventured close. One day, driven by an inner urge, she approached the scales with a singular intention: to weigh her deeds and see their reflection in the waters of Jivana.

Gently placing a token representing her actions on one side of the scale, she observed the other side. Instead of a direct reflection of her deeds, it bore the weight of her intentions, emotions, and the ripple effects of her actions. To her astonishment, the deeds she believed were trivial had caused profound ripples, and some grand gestures had barely left a mark.

Pondering this enigma, an elderly sage, Samsaravajra, who had been observing from a distance, approached her. "Child," he began, "The scales of Jivana don't operate on our linear understanding of deeds. They weigh the essence, the core of our actions. The universe resonates not with what we do, but how and why we do it."

Seeking clarity, Tsultrim queried, "How do I ensure that my deeds bear the right weight?"

Samsaravajra, smiling kindly, replied, "Seek not to act for the reflection you desire in the river but act with purity of intention, understanding, and compassion. The scales and the river merely mirror the cosmic dance of cause and effect. Be mindful, for every action, seen or unseen, echoes in the vast cosmos."

Conclusion:
The tale of the Golden Scales of Jivana serves as a profound reflection on the nuanced dance of karma. Beyond the visible realm of actions lies the vast expanse of intentions, emotions, and cosmic echoes. The narrative encourages introspection, challenging the reader to go beyond the superficiality of deeds, diving deep into the realm of intentions. For in this exploration lies the essence of true

understanding, where actions and their cosmic reverberations harmoniously coalesce.

THE CHAINED CHALICE OF VIMUKTI

In the heart of the ethereal mountains of Jiuhua, a secret cavern known as Atman resided. Inside this cavern stood a pedestal bearing a chalice named Vimukti. This chalice was no ordinary vessel; it was chained to the ground and was said to contain the elixir of enlightenment. Yet, the chains would only be released for the one who truly understood the dance of Karma.

Anala, a wise yet humble monk from the distant plains of Dhvani, had devoted his life to seeking this very elixir. He had heard whispers of the Chained Chalice and, after many moons of searching, stood at the entrance of Atman.

With every step inside the cavern, memories of his past deeds, intentions, and the subsequent ripples they caused in the world emerged before his eyes. The dance of cause and effect, every action and reaction intertwined in a cosmic ballet, played out before him.

As he approached Vimukti, he felt the weight of his entire life – the harmony and discord of his actions and their outcomes. Realization dawned upon Anala that mere physical chains didn't bind the chalice but by the intricate web of Karma.

In profound contemplation, Anala closed his eyes and dived deep within himself. He revisited every deed, not with guilt or pride, but with understanding and compassion. He embraced his imperfections, celebrated his growth, and sent forth an intention of love and gratitude for all experiences, for they shaped his journey.

Upon opening his eyes, Anala witnessed the chains dissolve into a luminous mist. The Chalice of Vimukti, now free, floated toward him. As he took a sip of the elixir, waves of enlightenment cascaded through him, and the dance of Karma revealed itself in its entirety.

Conclusion:

The journey to the Chained Chalice of Vimukti is a symbolic pilgrimage into the depths of one's own actions and intentions. It's a testament to the intricate and delicate interplay of cause and effect, reminding us that enlightenment isn't a mere destination but an understanding of this dance. Every action, every thought, every intention is a link in the boundless chain of existence. True liberation, or Vimukti, lies not in renouncing this dance but in embracing, understanding, and harmonizing with it.

THE REFLECTIVE ORCHARD OF PADMA

In the serene village of Padma, where time itself seemed to meditate, a mystical garden named Vimana was the heart of all tales. In this garden, blooms were not of petals and fragrance but of one's own actions, manifested and reflected.

Nalin, a seeker of truths, ventured into Vimana, drawn by its legends. The entrance bore an inscription: "Here, seeds of actions bear the fruits of destiny."

Within Vimana, Nalin found trees bearing fruits of every kind. But these were no ordinary trees. Each was a reflection of an individual's life, showcasing their deeds and the ripples they sent forth into the cosmos.

One tree bore withered fruits, another blossomed with radiant orbs, and yet another bore fruits that transformed from withered to radiant as he observed. Nalin, intrigued, found a sapling with his own name inscribed at its base.

The sapling bore a mix of vibrant and withered fruits. Picking up a withered one, he was instantly flooded with a memory: a thoughtless word spoken in anger to a dear friend. The radiant fruit revealed a moment when he offered solace to a troubled stranger.

Realizing that the trees mirrored the dance of Karma, Nalin sat in meditation. He delved deep, reconciling with his past actions, understanding their profound implications, and setting forth intentions of mindfulness and compassion for the journey ahead.

Days turned into nights and nights into days, until one dawn, Nalin emerged from his meditation to find his sapling transformed. It was now a radiant tree, balanced in its manifestations, reflecting harmony with the dance of cause and effect.

As Nalin exited Vimana, the garden whispered a profound truth: "In the tapestry of existence, every thread, every action, interweaves with another, crafting the grand design of destiny."

Conclusion:
Vimana, the Garden of Reflections, serves as a profound mirror, reflecting the intricacies of the dance of Karma. Every action, intentional or unconscious, casts ripples in the vast sea of existence. The narrative beckons one to introspect, to understand the weight and resonance of their actions, and to walk the path of life with heightened awareness. For in this heightened consciousness lies the

key to harmonizing with the cosmic dance, realizing that our every act, thought, and intention contributes to the grand choreography of existence.

THE RIVER OF SAMSARA

Deep within the lush valleys of Dharma, a river flowed with mesmerizing grace. Its waters, however, were not merely elements but shimmered with the experiences of souls. This was the River of Samsara.

Mihira, a young mendicant with eyes searching for deeper truths, came upon this river during her wanderings. She noticed that every ripple, every current within the river seemed to echo with memories, desires, and karmic imprints.

Beside the river stood an ancient banyan tree, its roots drinking deeply from Samsara's waters. Taking shade under it, Mihira closed her eyes, only to be transported into the river's flow.

She found herself in its currents, witnessing myriad life scenarios play out: joyous unions, heart-wrenching separations, acts of kindness, betrayals, creation, and destruction. Each scene morphed into another, tied not by chronology but by an intricate web of actions and their outcomes.

A realization dawned upon Mihira: The river did not flow linearly from a source to a destination. Instead, it flowed cyclically, where cause merged into effect, and effect became the cause for another cycle. The patterns repeated, sometimes amplifying and at other times diminishing, but always in a loop.

Emerging from her meditation, Mihira saw a boat anchored nearby with an oar inscribed, "Mindful Intent." Embarking upon it, she started rowing with deep introspection and purpose.

As she rowed with conscious intentions and a genuine understanding of her actions, she began navigating the Samsara currents. She realized that while she couldn't control the entire river, she could steer her boat, shaping her journey within its cyclical flow.

Mihira's boat eventually found a serene bank – a space of enlightenment where the cyclical currents of Samsara transformed into a vast, tranquil ocean of Nirvana.

Conclusion:

The River of Samsara is a profound metaphor for the cyclical nature of Karma - how our actions, thoughts, and intentions flow into the universe, influencing and being influenced in return. Mihira's journey underscores the power of mindful intent. While we may not control the vast expanse of life's experiences, we hold the oar of intentionality to navigate and influence our journey. By understanding and harmonizing with the law of cause and effect, one can transcend the cyclical torrents of Samsara and find the peaceful shores of enlightenment.

THE SYMPHONY OF COSMIC ECHOES

In a realm untouched by time, where silence hummed the eternal tunes of the cosmos, stood the Mountain of Echoes, Ananta. This mountain was not made of rock and soil but of vibrations of actions sent forth by beings from all of existence.

A sage named Nirvanash, whose spirit danced to the beats of cosmic wisdom, was drawn to Ananta, sensing its celestial symphony. His soul yearned to understand the melodies that intertwined with the strings of the universe.

As Nirvanash stepped onto Ananta, he could hear the echoes of myriad actions, some a sweet melody, others a cacophonous discord. Each echo seemed to send forth ripples, intertwining with other echoes, creating an ever-evolving symphony.

Nirvanash sat in contemplation, immersing his being in the vibrations of Ananta. He observed how each harmonic echo spread its essence, touching other echoes and blending into new harmonies or dissonances.

He saw actions of love and kindness resonate with beautiful harmony, their echoes interweaving with others to create a divine melody. Conversely, actions of harm and deceit clashed in discord, their echoes disrupting the celestial harmony.

It dawned upon Nirvanash that these were not mere echoes but representations of the Law of Karma. Every action and every intention sent forth its echo, and these echoes shaped the symphony of existence.

A deeper realization embraced Nirvanash. The Symphony was not precomposed; it was being created every moment, with every echo. He understood the potential each being held to contribute to celestial harmony through mindful and righteous actions.

With newfound wisdom, Nirvanash descended from Ananta, his every step, his every breath in sync with the cosmic symphony. He became a beacon of harmonic resonance, guiding others to realize their role in crafting the eternal Symphony of Cosmic Echoes.

Conclusion:

Ananta, the Mountain of Echoes, symbolizes the intertwining and everlasting nature of actions in the cosmic symphony. Nirvanash's realization offers profound insight into the essence of Karma, highlighting how every action and every thought sends forth its echo in the vast cosmos. The harmonious and discordant echoes represent the righteous and harmful actions, showing their impact on the universal symphony. This story invites the reader to reflect upon their actions, to realize their potential in contributing to the celestial harmony, and to live with the understanding that each echo they send forth shapes the eternal dance of the cosmos. By embracing righteous and mindful living, one can resonate with the divine melodies of existence and inspire others to join in the harmonious symphony of the universe.

THE GARDEN OF IMPRINTS

In a village nestled at the foot of the Vipassana Mountains, there was a garden unlike any other, known to the locals as Bodhi Vana. This garden did not bear flowers, fruits, or trees. Instead, it bore imprints.

At the dawn of their understanding, each villager would visit this garden and find a patch of earth waiting for them. Every action, every word, every thought they ever had would leave an imprint on this ground.

A noble act would birth a luminous imprint, radiant and pulsating with light. A harmful deed, in contrast, would cast a shadowy, dense mark. As days turned into years, the patches of earth became intricate tapestries of imprints.

Dhara, a seeker of wisdom, often visited Bodhi Vana. Through her meditative gaze, she discerned the patterns woven by the imprints. She realized the interconnection of actions, where each imprint influenced the creation of the next. A luminous mark often birthed more luminous marks, while shadowy imprints led to further obscurations.

One day, as Dhara sat deep in contemplation, she saw a peculiar phenomenon. A dense shadowy imprint was surrounded by a cluster of luminous ones. Over time, this shadow began to lighten, eventually transforming into a radiant imprint.

Moved by this transformation, Dhara realized the true essence of Karma. While every action left an indelible imprint, the present moment held the power to influence the nature of future imprints. Through mindful actions and intent, one could shift from shadow to luminosity.

With this profound understanding, Dhara began her journey, guiding villagers to cultivate their patches mindfully. She taught them that while the past shaped their present, their present had the profound power to sculpt their future.

Conclusion:
Bodhi Vana serves as a mirror to the cosmos, where every action resonates with the Law of Karma, leaving imprints in the vast tapestry of existence. Dhara's observation of the transformation of imprints reinforces the notion that one's present actions, when grounded in mindfulness and righteousness, can transmute the consequences of past deeds. The story beckons the reader to introspect on their own tapestry of life, urging them to cultivate it with care, awareness, and noble intentions. It underscores that

while we are products of our past, we are also the architects of our future. Through understanding and wisdom, one can weave a life that not only resonates with luminosity for oneself but also illuminates the path for others.

The Ego and Humility

Throughout our lives, the dynamics of ego and humility play critical roles in shaping our interactions and personal growth. Here we vividly illustrate the journey from ego-driven actions to humble realizations, reflecting the philosophies of Buddhism, Taoism, and Ikigai. By understanding these principles, we are encouraged to live with greater self-awareness and balance, recognizing the transformative power of humility.

Buddhism: Transcending the Ego

In Buddhism, humility is viewed as a virtue essential for spiritual growth and enlightenment. The ego, characterized by self-importance and pride, is seen as a barrier to true understanding and compassion. Humility, on the other hand, opens the mind to learning and self-awareness, enabling individuals to perceive the true nature of reality.

Buddhism teaches that the ego, or the sense of a separate self, is a major source of suffering. The ego clings to desires, aversions, and illusions of control, leading to a cycle of discontent and suffering. By cultivating humility and letting go of the ego, one can achieve inner peace and enlightenment.

In the stories within this chapter, characters often face the consequences of ego-driven actions and find liberation through humility. For instance, "The Bamboo and the Oak" illustrates how a proud character learns the value of humility by observing the resilience of the humble bamboo.

In "The Ego and the Essence" explores the idea that the ego obscures our true nature and potential. The characters in the story learn that by letting go of their ego-driven desires and actions, they can connect with their true essence and achieve greater fulfillment and peace.

Buddhism emphasizes that the ego is a barrier to enlightenment. By practicing mindfulness and self-awareness, individuals can transcend their ego and connect with their true essence. This tale highlights the transformative power of humility and self-awareness in the journey towards enlightenment.

Similarly, "The Mountain and the Grain of Sand" contrasts the grandiosity of the mountain with the humility of the grain of sand. The story illustrates that even the smallest and seemingly insignificant elements have value and purpose. This perspective helps individuals see beyond their own ego and appreciate the broader context of their actions.

Buddhist teachings encourage individuals to see the value in all beings and actions, regardless of their apparent size or importance. This story reinforces the idea that humility allows us to appreciate the interconnectedness of all things and recognize the value in every action and being.

Taoism: The Balance of Ego and Humility

Central to Taoist teachings are the virtues of compassion, moderation, and humility, known as the Three Treasures.

Taoism emphasizes the importance of balance and harmony, teaching that true wisdom lies in humility and simplicity. The ego, with its desires and ambitions, disrupts the natural flow of the Tao. By embracing humility and aligning with the Tao, one can live in harmony with the universe.

"The Unseen Balance" is a tale that embodies the Taoist principle of harmony and humility. The characters in this story learn to find peace by aligning their actions with the natural order, recognizing that true balance and harmony come from living in accordance with the Tao. This story highlights how humility allows individuals to flow with the natural rhythms of life, avoiding the disruptions caused by ego and pride.

In "The Pottery of Fate," characters discover that their actions, when aligned with the natural order, bring about harmony and success. Conversely, actions driven by greed and ego lead to imbalance and misfortune. This tale reflects the Taoist belief in wu wei, or effortless action, where humility and a lack of forced effort lead to natural and harmonious outcomes. The story teaches that humility allows individuals to act in tune with the Tao, avoiding the pitfalls of ego-driven decisions.

"The Weaver and the King" tells of a ruler who learns the importance of humility through the teachings of a simple weaver. This story reflects the Taoist ideal that humility leads to wisdom and peace.

In "The Tale of the Silent Mountain," a character discovers the power of quiet strength and inner stillness, embodying the Taoist principle that true power comes from humility and alignment with the natural order.

Ikigai: Humble Purpose and Fulfillment

In Japanese culture, humility is a deeply ingrained value, often seen as a sign of strength and wisdom rather than weakness. This cultural emphasis on humility complements the pursuit of Ikigai, as it encourages individuals to recognize their place within a larger community and to act with consideration for others.

Humility in the context of Ikigai involves understanding and accepting one's strengths and limitations, being open to continuous learning, and valuing the contributions of others. It discourages ego-driven actions and promotes a sense of interconnectedness and mutual respect.

Ikigai, integrates humility as a crucial element in discovering and living one's true purpose. It suggests that by letting go of ego and embracing humility, one can find deeper fulfillment and contribute meaningfully to the world.

In "The Feather and the Stone," a character discovers their Ikigai by focusing on the humble act of teaching others, finding profound satisfaction in this selfless pursuit. This narrative aligns with the Ikigai principle that true fulfillment comes from living a life of purpose and humility.

The Lake of Mirrored Souls: This tale explores how characters confront their egos and find peace through humility. It illustrates that letting go of ego-driven desires leads to deeper connections and self-understanding.

THE LAKE OF MIRRORED SOULS

In the heart of Jhanapada, where the air hums with whispered secrets of the cosmos, there is a serene lake known as Atma Jala. Its waters, clearer than the vast skies, hold a unique power; they reflect not the physical form but the inner soul of any being that gaze upon its surface.

Rajana, a scholar of great renown, having heard tales of this lake, journeyed to its shores, driven by curiosity. Over the years, with the acclaim and respect he had garnered, a subtle pride had taken root in him. As he stood at the water's edge, the lake revealed a stormy and turbulent reflection, indicating the tempest of his inflated ego.

Beside him was an old mendicant, Vimala, with eyes that held the calm of countless monsoons. She gazed into the lake, and her reflection was that of a tranquil and vast expanse, mirroring her humility and inner peace.

Intrigued by the stark difference in their reflections, Rajana humbled himself to ask Vimala about hers. With a gentle smile, she narrated her journey from ego to humility, from a tempestuous storm to a serene calm. She spoke of moments when pride had blinded her, of times when she had believed she was the doer of her deeds, and the universe revolved around her will.

It was only when she truly observed the interconnectedness of all things, recognizing the vast web in which each action, each being, and each thought was but a mere thread, that she found true humility. "In understanding our insignificance, we find our true significance," she whispered.

The profoundness of Vimala's words made Rajana introspect deeply. He sat by the lake, meditating on his ego, letting the waters of Atma Jala cleanse his soul. Days turned into nights, and nights into days. When he finally stood up and gazed into the lake, he saw a calmer reflection, not as tranquil as Vimala's, but on a path towards it.

Conclusion:

Atma Jala, with its mystical reflections, portrays the journey of the soul through the maze of ego and humility. Rajana's turbulent reflection is emblematic of the inner chaos that ego breeds, while Vimala's serene expanse represents the peace and vastness that humility brings. The story emphasizes that ego confines, blinds, and isolates, whereas humility liberates, enlightens, and connects. By recognizing our place in the vast interconnected web of existence, we can move from the storm of self-centeredness to the tranquility of selflessness. This tale invites the reader to reflect upon their own inner waters, to discern the storms and calms, and to embark on a journey from ego to true humility.

THE BAMBOO AND THE OAK

In the village of Dhammavijaya, where the winds carried tales of wisdom and compassion, there stood side by side a grand oak tree and a slender bamboo. The oak, with its vast canopy and thick trunk, took great pride in its stature, often boasting about its strength and age to the neighboring trees.

The bamboo, though much younger and less grand in appearance, remained silent, swaying gracefully with the winds, never uttering a word of comparison or envy.

One day, a traveling monk named Yatiko came to rest under the trees. Observing the oak's proud demeanor and the bamboo's quiet elegance, he asked, "O magnificent oak and graceful bamboo, if the heavens were to unleash a mighty storm upon this land, who amongst you would stand tall when dawn breaks?"

The oak, without a moment's hesitation, responded, "I, with my strength and deep roots, have weathered many storms. I shall stand tall, as I always have."

The bamboo, with a soft rustle, replied, "I know not of the morrow, but I shall bend with the winds, bow to the forces, and hope to stand once they pass."

As fate would have it, that very night, a fierce storm raged upon Dhammavijaya. The oak stood firm, resisting the powerful gusts, its branches battling the winds. The bamboo, on the other hand, bent gracefully, allowing the winds to pass over and through.

As dawn broke, the villagers awoke to a sight of despair. The mighty oak, which had resisted the storm with all its might, lay uprooted, its grandeur lost to the ravages of the night. Next to it, the bamboo stood tall, albeit a few leaves shorter, having danced with the winds and embraced the storm.

Conclusion:
The oak and the bamboo offer profound insights into the nature of ego and humility. With its unyielding pride, the oak believed itself invincible, only to be felled by the very strength it clung to. In its humility, the bamboo recognized its vulnerability and used it as a strength, bending rather than breaking.
This tale is a gentle reminder that sometimes, true strength lies not in standing tall and resisting but in bending and adapting. The rigidity of ego can often lead to our downfall, whereas the flexibility of humility can pave the way for enduring grace. As we face the

storms of life, may we learn to dance with the winds, like the bamboo, rather than resist them in vain pride, like the oak.

THE EGO AND THE ESSENCE

In the heart of the kingdom of Suddhanapura, where wisdom whispered through every leaf and stone, two reflecting entities resided: a polished, golden mirror and a vast, serene lake.

The golden mirror was the prized possession of the kingdom's most affluent merchant. It was said that the mirror could reflect the beauty of anything that stood before it with unparalleled clarity. People from distant lands would visit the merchant's palace, offering riches just for a momentary glimpse of their reflection, accentuated by the mirror's golden touch.

The lake, on the other hand, lay quietly at the edge of the kingdom, its expansive waters reflecting the skies, mountains, birds, and the daily life of Suddhanapura. It asked for nothing yet provided for many, serving as a source of life, sustenance, and contemplation.

One day, a curious sage, Pannasila, journeyed to the kingdom. Having heard tales of both reflectors, he sought to understand the essence of true reflection. He first approached the grand mirror in the merchant's palace.

"O splendid mirror," Pannasila inquired, "what do you see?"

"I reflect perfection," the mirror responded with pride. "I show the world as it wishes to be seen. In me, everyone finds a more beautiful version of themselves."

Pannasila then traveled to the tranquil shores of the lake and posed the same question, "O boundless lake, what do you see?"

"I see life," replied the lake with a gentle ripple. "In my depths and surfaces, I reflect the world as it is - the fleeting clouds, the soaring birds, the changing seasons, the joy, and the sorrow. I don't add, nor do I subtract. I am but a canvas for the universe's ever-changing art."

Conclusion:

The tale presents to us a profound juxtaposition of ego and humility. In its confined splendor, the mirror shows a selective, often embellished reflection, feeding the ego and catering to one's desire for validation. The lake, vast and unassuming, mirrors the world in its entirety, embodying humility and authenticity.

This tale beckons us to ponder: In the pursuit of self-awareness, would we rather be a mirror, reflecting what's convenient and flattering, or be like the lake, reflecting with honesty and depth?

The world's true essence is not in selective portrayals but in embracing the entirety of existence with humility and grace.

THE MOUNTAIN AND THE GRAIN OF SAND

In the realm of Anupama, two contrasting existences were present: An imposing mountain known as Girikandra and a diminutive grain of sand, Sushiksha.

Girikandra, towering above all, wore a cloak of snow at its peak and was adorned with trees, cascading waterfalls, and inhabited by myriad creatures. Its majestic presence was so awe-inspiring that pilgrims traveled from distant lands just to cast a reverent gaze upon it. Girikandra, aware of its magnitude and grandeur, often mused, "I am the symbol of might and permanence. All beings look up to me, both literally and figuratively."

Sushiksha, on the other hand, lay humbly on the vast shorelines of river Ananya. It was a mere dot in the vast expanse, indistinguishable among billions of other grains. Yet, it harbored a quiet understanding of its place in the grand tapestry of existence. It thought, "I am minuscule, a tiny fragment of the universe, yet I am part of the grand whole."

A sage, Vidura, having heard of the mountain's reputation and intrigued by the unnoticed existence of the grain of sand, embarked on a journey to converse with both.

To Girikandra, he asked, "Mighty Mountain, how do you view your existence?"

With a sense of pride, Girikandra responded, "I stand tall, timeless, witnessing the epochs of the world. Every creature looks to me for shelter and inspiration. I am unparalleled."

Vidura then approached the grain of sand and whispered, "Dear Sushiksha, how do you perceive your being amidst this vast universe?"

With a gentle sense of acceptance, Sushiksha replied, "I am but a fleeting moment in the endless dance of time. Yet, I hold within me the essence of the entire universe. In my insignificance, I find my true significance."

Conclusion:
The mountain, in its pride, represents the towering ego many harbors, believing in their unparalleled significance. The grain of sand, Sushiksha, embodies the humility in understanding one's tiny but essential place in the cosmos. The true essence of existence is not in dominating landscapes but in acknowledging our transient nature while recognizing the universe within. Through introspection, one should seek to diminish the imposing mountain of ego and embody the

humility of the grain of sand, understanding that real strength lies in the acceptance of one's place within the grand scheme.

THE WEAVER AND THE KING

In the tranquil town of Dhammaville, there lived a humble weaver named Santikaro. His skill was unparalleled, but he took no pride in his talents, working diligently day after day to produce intricate cloth of the highest quality.

Not far from the town, in an opulent palace, resided King Mahendra, who was renowned not just for his vast kingdom but also for his towering ego. His shadow of arrogance was so pervasive that it darkened the hearts of his subjects.

One day, a courtier presented King Mahendra with a robe made by Santikaro. It was so exquisite that the fabric seemed to be spun from the rays of the morning sun. Intrigued and slightly envious of the weaver's skill, the King summoned Santikaro to his court.

As Santikaro entered, the courtiers whispered among themselves, awed by the masterpiece he had created. But Santikaro's demeanor was calm, his head bowed in humility.

King Mahendra, trying to impose his superiority, said, "They say you are the best weaver in all of Dhammaville. Tell me, Santikaro, do you believe you are better than everyone else?"

Santikaro replied gently, "Your Majesty, I simply weave. The quality of the cloth is not a testament to my greatness but to the teachings I've received and the divine that works through my hands."

Unsettled and intrigued, King Mahendra challenged Santikaro to a weaving competition. He called upon the royal weavers, and a contest was set: They were to create a fabric depicting the essence of life.

Days passed. With their vast resources, the royal weavers created a cloth shimmering with gold and adorned with precious stones. It showed the King in his majesty, ruling over vast landscapes and heavens.

Santikaro, on the other hand, wove a simple scene: A vast, expansive sky with a rising sun on one end and a setting sun on the other. In the middle, under a Bodhi tree, sat a meditative figure radiating a calm glow.

When the clothes were presented, the court was divided. The King's ministers praised the royal weaver's creation, highlighting its opulence. But a wise old advisor stepped forward and said, "The royal weavers have indeed depicted the magnificence of the King, but Santikaro has depicted the magnificence of life itself."

King Mahendra, deep down, recognized the truth in the advisor's words. He asked Santikaro, "How did you envision such a scene?"

Santikaro replied, "Your Majesty, life is transient. It's not the riches or the power one holds but the inner peace and understanding of the impermanence of everything."

Conclusion:
In the vast tapestry of life, it's not the external accolades and material gains that define our essence. Santikaro's cloth, in its simplicity, challenged the conventional notions of grandeur. It beckoned one to look beyond the tangible and delve into the intangible realms of inner peace and enlightenment. The ego, represented by King Mahendra, often blinds us, making us believe in our invincibility. But true strength and understanding come from humility, from recognizing the greater forces at play, and from embracing the transient nature of life.

THE TALE OF THE SILENT MOUNTAIN

In a land cloaked in the whisper of breezes and the murmur of streams, there resided a mountain, ancient and wise, named Sannidhi. Sannidhi had watched empires rise and fall had felt the breath of countless seasons brush against its peaks. Yet, despite its ancientness, it was not proud; it spoke in the language of silence, and its wisdom was open to all who sought it.

Within the same realm, the river Taranga flowed with a loud and proud voice. She believed her ceaseless movement, her ability to shape the land, was a symbol of her superiority over the static, silent mountain.

The creatures of the land, torn between the silent wisdom of the mountain and the loud pride of the river, often pondered over who was greater. One day, the creatures decided to approach Sannidhi and Taranga to settle this query.

The mountain, in its eternal silence, whispered the truth of existence in the ears of the wind, which carried it to every being in the realm. "In the stillness, in the quiet, wisdom blooms. The loudness of self-importance is but a fleeting ripple in the eternal pond of existence. True strength lies not in proclaiming one's greatness but in the humble acceptance of one's place in the cosmos."

Taranga, on the other hand, scoffed and swirled, proclaiming, "Look at the lands I nourish, the civilizations I cradle. My currents shape the earth. I am the bringer of life, the shaper of destinies!"

The creatures listened, feeling the silent wisdom of Sannidhi seeping into their souls and the loud assertions of Taranga brushing against their senses. They pondered upon the contrast between the silent humility of the mountain and the vocal arrogance of the river. In the quiet whisper of Sannidhi, they found the eternal truths of existence, the quiet acceptance of one's place in the vast tapestry of life.

Conclusion:

In this allegorical tale, Sannidhi, the silent mountain, symbolizes the profound and humble truth that exists within the quiet acceptance of oneself and the universe's grand design. The ego, symbolized by the loud and proud river Taranga, blinds one with self-importance, distancing one from the profound truths of existence.

The silent wisdom of the mountain whispers to us the importance of humility and the acceptance of the grand symphony of existence in which we are but a single note. It invites us to peel away the layers of our ego, to embrace the quiet, the stillness within us, and to listen to the subtle whispers of the universe.

In contrast, the loud proclamations of the river urge us to reflect upon the transience of self-importance and the illusions it cast upon our perception of existence. It is a reminder not to let the clamor of self-importance drown out the harmonious symphony of silent wisdom.

The creatures of the land, akin to seekers of truth, are left to reflect upon and choose between the silent, profound wisdom and the loud, transient self-importance. This tale is a gentle nudge to embrace humility, to seek the silent wisdom within, and to align oneself with the harmonious dance of the cosmos. It is an invitation to transcend the loudness of ego and to embrace the silent symphony of humble existence.

THE FEATHER AND THE STONE

In the heart of a vast and serene forest, a curious dialogue took place between a floating feather and a resting stone. Both lay at the base of a grand old tree, having experienced different paths through the forest.

The feather began, "See how gracefully I have journeyed through the forest, dancing with the wind, touching the heavens, and caressing the treetops. The sky is familiar with my elegance, and the earth admires my lightness."

The stone listened patiently and then replied, "Indeed, your journey has been beautiful, full of movement and wonder. I've witnessed much from this very spot, nestled in the earth. I've felt the embrace of the soil, the touch of rain, and the warmth of sunlight. Though I don't soar as you do, I know the depth and stability of the land."

The feather, with a hint of pride, said, "But you remain here, grounded and still, while I experience freedom and the vastness of the world."

The stone, in its calm demeanor, responded, "True freedom, dear feather, is not just in flight but in knowing one's nature and being at peace with it. While you glide in the air, I am content with my stillness. Every grain of my being resonates with the stories of this forest, and in my stability, I find profound freedom."

Days turned into nights, and seasons changed. One day, a turbulent storm approached. The feather, having nothing to hold onto, was carried away, lost amidst the fury of the wind. The stone, however, remained undisturbed, continuing its quiet communion with the forest.

When the storm subsided, the feather returned, worn and weary, and settled next to the stone. It spoke with a newfound humility, "In my pride of flight, I overlooked the strength in stillness, the wisdom in rootedness. Your quiet strength and humility have taught me the value of knowing oneself beyond external validations."

The stone gently replied, "Each of us has a role in the grand tapestry of existence. Ego blinds us with comparisons and ranks, but humility teaches us to appreciate the beauty in every path, whether it's in the vastness of the sky or the depth of the earth."

Conclusion:

This tale brings forth the essence of humility and the illusion of ego. With its ability to soar, the feather represents the ego that often blinds us with pride and comparison. The stone, grounded and stable, embodies humility, rooted in self-awareness and contentment.

The storm is a metaphor for life's challenges that test our true nature. In the face of adversity, ego wavers, but humility stands firm, deriving strength from inner understanding rather than external achievements.

Through the interplay between the feather and the stone, we are reminded that true wisdom lies not in boasting of one's capabilities but in recognizing and respecting the inherent value in all paths. It's a call to transcend the confines of ego and embrace the expansive realm of humility, where every being, every journey, has its unique significance and beauty.

THE TALE OF THE SUN AND THE MOON

In a realm beyond time, where the heavens paint stories of cosmic wisdom, the Sun and the Moon engaged in a rare celestial conversation. Both luminous beings played pivotal roles in the eternal dance of the cosmos, yet their existences were starkly contrasting spectacles of the Universe's profound mysteries.

With its blazing splendor, the Sun remarked, "Look at the vast universe reveling in my radiance. I am the bringer of light and life. My brilliance fuels the world, drives the darkness away, and paints the day with my golden hues."

The Moon, bathed in gentle silver light, responded quietly, "Your radiance is indeed magnificent. It sustains life and brings energy to the cosmos. I, however, reflect the subtle light in the silence of the night, illuminating the dark sky with my soft glow, whispering the secrets of the unseen to the world below."

In its radiant confidence, the Sun said, "But your light is borrowed; it is my light that you reflect. I am the source, the originator of energy."

The Moon, with serene humility, replied, "Indeed, your light is the source, and I am but a mirror. Yet, in this quiet reflection, the world finds solace and beauty in the stillness of the night, sees the universe's whispering essence, and understands the value of subtlety and silence."

The eternal waltz continued, with days bathed in golden brilliance and nights swathed in silver whispers. One such day, a total eclipse occurred, a rare celestial dance where the Moon crossed paths with the Sun, cloaking it in her shadow. It was in this momentary embrace that the Sun experienced the tranquil beauty of the Moon's silent wisdom.

When the dance concluded, and the Sun once again bathed the cosmos in its golden light, it spoke with newfound respect, "In our fleeting union, I felt the profound beauty in your silent wisdom, the peace in your soft glow. I now see the strength in quiet reflection and the grace in silent illumination."

The Moon, with her gentle light, replied, "And I am ever grateful for your radiant energy, allowing me to share the hidden beauty of the cosmos with the world. We are harmonious contrasts, reflections of the infinite wisdom and diversity of the universe."

Conclusion:

This allegorical tale of the Sun and the Moon is a gentle reminder of the interplay between ego and humility. The Sun, with its overwhelming brilliance and life-giving energy, symbolizes the ego's power and influence. It shines with self-assurance, its light essential yet blinding, overshadowing the subtle beauties of existence. Conversely, the Moon represents humility. It doesn't claim originality but reflects the light bestowed upon it, showcasing the unseen and the overlooked, the silent whispers of the cosmos, and the soothing tranquility of the night.

The momentary union during the eclipse symbolizes the transformative realization, a fleeting glimpse into the harmonious existence of contrasts, the dance of light and shadow, brilliance and subtlety. It's a poignant reminder that humility is not the absence of power but the recognition and acceptance of one's place in the vast tapestry of existence.

In this profound understanding, one finds the strength to see beyond the blinding self and embrace the diverse beauties and wisdom the universe offers, learning to be a silent observer, a reflective learner, and a harmonious part of the cosmic dance. The tale invites us to transcend the self-centric view and to embrace the expansive and inclusive perspective of cosmic harmony, where ego and humility coexist and complement, painting the universe with varied strokes of celestial wisdom.

THE ORCHID AND THE OAK

In the lush heart of an ancient forest, where nature whispered tales of time and the delicate dance of life, stood a magnificent Oak. With its expansive canopy, sturdy trunk, and sprawling roots, the Oak was the monarch of the woodland, towering over its fellow inhabitants with pride and authority.

Near the base of this grand tree grew a delicate Orchid. Its slender stem, fragile petals, and soft hues made it almost invisible against the forest's grandeur. Yet, those who ventured close enough found in it a beauty so subtle and profound that it captured the heart and soul.

One day, the Oak, looking down upon the Orchid, said, "Why do you grow here, little flower? My vast shadow cloaks your beauty, and my mighty roots deprive you of nourishment. In the shadow of my greatness, you remain insignificant."

The Orchid, with its gentle demeanor, responded, "Great Oak, I grow here not to compete with your grandeur but to complement it. Your strength offers me protection, and your shade provides me with the subtle light I need. In your vastness, I find my purpose."

The Oak scoffed, "Purpose? I stand tall, sheltering the creatures, marking the passage of time, and holding the earth beneath. While you, with your fragile existence, what purpose do you hold?"

The Orchid whispered, "I exist to remind all that beauty and strength are not just in grand gestures and towering presences. They are also in the subtle whispers, the fleeting moments, the delicate balances. I am a testament to the idea that one can find purpose and meaning even in the smallest of existences."

Seasons changed, and a great storm approached the forest. The trees braced themselves against the raging winds, but the Oak, in all its might, was uprooted, its grandeur brought down in one swift motion.

The forest mourned the loss of its monarch, but life, as it always does, moved on. The space where the Oak once stood was now bathed in light, and where its roots had once sprawled now lay fertile ground.

The Orchid, sensing the change, began to bloom in a way it never had before. Its petals radiated colors more vibrant, its fragrance more intoxicating. And around it, more orchids began to grow, painting the forest floor in a mosaic of colors, a testament to life's resilience and nature's balance.

Conclusion:
The tale of the Orchid and the Oak provides a mirror to our understanding of ego and humility. The Oak, representing the ego, stands tall, its grandeur undeniable. It measures worth by size, strength, and presence. The Orchid, on the other hand, symbolizes humility. Delicate yet resilient, it finds its purpose not in overshadowing others but in complementing them.

The storm signifies the unpredictable nature of life, where even the mightiest can fall. In the aftermath, the Orchid's blooming is a poignant reminder that true strength often lies not in towering over others but in understanding one's place in the vast tapestry of existence.

The tale challenges the conventional belief that greatness is synonymous with grandeur. It invites the reader to find beauty in subtlety, strength in humility, and purpose in every existence, no matter how small or fragile. For, in the dance of life, every entity, grand or subtle, has a part to play, a story to tell, and a lesson to impart.

THE STONE CUTTER'S DESIRE

In a small village nestled between two mountains, there lived a stone cutter named Tenzin. Every day, Tenzin would diligently chip away at the giant boulders, crafting beautiful statues and ornaments that the villagers admired. However, in his heart, Tenzin felt a burning discontent. He wished for more power, more recognition, and a life greater than that of a simple stone cutter.

One hot afternoon, while Tenzin was working under the unforgiving sun, he exclaimed, "How mighty the sun is! I wish I were the sun, reigning over everything and everyone." To his astonishment, his wish was granted, and he found himself glowing fiercely in the sky, looking down upon the earth.

As the sun, Tenzin shone brilliantly, scorching the fields and causing the villagers to seek shelter from his intense heat. He felt powerful, watching the world dance to his whims.

However, soon, a massive cloud moved, shielding the earth from his rays. Tenzin thought, "This cloud holds more power than I, blocking my light. I wish to be the cloud."

Once again, his wish was granted. As the cloud, he poured rain upon the village, causing floods and chaos. He reveled in his newfound might, but this was short-lived. The strong winds soon pushed him, tossing him here and there without resistance. "The wind is mightier than I. I wish to be the wind!" Tenzin exclaimed.

Transformed into the wind, Tenzin blew ferociously, uprooting trees and destroying homes. Yet, as he attempted to move a giant mountain, he found himself powerless. The mountain stood firm, unaffected by his gusts. "This mountain is mightier. I wish to be the mountain," Tenzin wished.

Now, as the mountain, Tenzin felt invincible. Nothing could move him; he stood tall and majestic. But as days turned into nights, he felt something chipping away at his base. It was a stone cutter, just like him, molding the mountain into shapes and figures. "How can it be? A mere stone cutter has power over me. I wish to be a stone cutter again," Tenzin lamented.

In an instant, Tenzin was back in his familiar surroundings, holding his chisel and hammer. He felt a profound realization wash over him. No matter how much power he had, there would always be something more powerful, something beyond his control. True power, he realized, lay not in controlling others but in understanding one's place in the vast cycle of life.

Conclusion:

Tenzin's journey from a humble stone cutter to various powerful entities and back to his original self serves as a profound metaphor for the human ego's insatiable desire for power and recognition. The story illuminates the transient nature of power and the futility of chasing after it. True strength and wisdom lie in recognizing one's limitations, embracing humility, and finding contentment in one's role, no matter how big or small. The tale invites readers to reflect on their desires and understand that genuine fulfillment comes from inner peace and acceptance rather than external validation and dominance.

Acceptance of Change

Throughout our lives, change is an inevitable and constant force. The experience of change can be challenging, bringing with it uncertainty and disruption. However, it is through the acceptance of change that we find growth, resilience, and deeper understanding. Embracing change allows us to move forward, adapt, and thrive amidst life's shifting landscapes. The philosophies of Buddhism, Taoism, and Ikigai offer profound insights into how we can navigate and embrace change with grace and wisdom. By understanding these principles, we are encouraged to live with greater flexibility and resilience, recognizing that change is a fundamental aspect of life.

Change is essential because it drives personal growth and development. Every time we experience change, we learn something new about ourselves and the world around us. This process of learning and adaptation is crucial for personal growth. By embracing change, we become more flexible, adaptable, and resilient, which are essential traits for overcoming life's challenges and uncertainties. Changes can introduce us to new experiences, perspectives, and opportunities that we might have otherwise missed.

Embracing change also helps us break free from the monotony of routine. It encourages us to step out of our comfort zones and explore new possibilities, making life more interesting and fulfilling. Change brings a sense of adventure and excitement, allowing us to discover new passions and interests that enrich our lives.

From a psychological perspective, accepting change fosters a proactive mindset. When we embrace change, we take control of our lives and make conscious decisions that align with our goals and aspirations. This proactive approach helps us navigate life's uncertainties with confidence and purpose, ultimately leading to a more satisfying and meaningful life

Buddhism: Embracing Impermanence

Buddhism teaches that all things are impermanent and constantly changing. This understanding of impermanence, or anicca, is a cornerstone of Buddhist philosophy. It is one of the Three Marks of Existence (trilakkhana), along with dukkha (suffering) and anatta (non-self). By accepting the transient nature of life, reduces attachment and clinging, which are sources of suffering. Detachment is not indifference but a balanced, wise approach to life, achieving a state of peace and enlightenment.

Core Teachings of Anicca

- **EVERYTHING CHANGES:** ALL PHENOMENA, FROM THE SMALLEST PARTICLE TO THE VAST COSMOS, UNDERGO CONTINUOUS CHANGE. THIS INCLUDES OUR THOUGHTS, FEELINGS, AND PHYSICAL BODIES.
- **BIRTH, GROWTH, DECAY, AND DEATH:** THESE ARE THE STAGES THAT EVERY LIVING BEING AND MATERIAL OBJECT GO THROUGH. UNDERSTANDING THIS CYCLE HELPS IN ACCEPTING THE NATURAL

PROGRESSION OF LIFE AND REDUCES SUFFERING ASSOCIATED WITH LOSS AND DECAY.
- **MOMENTARINESS:** EVEN WITHIN A SEEMINGLY STABLE OBJECT OR EXPERIENCE, THERE IS CONSTANT CHANGE AT A MICRO-LEVEL. FOR EXAMPLE, OUR CELLS ARE CONSTANTLY BEING REPLACED, AND OUR THOUGHTS SHIFT FROM MOMENT TO MOMENT.

In the stories within this chapter, characters often face significant changes and learn to embrace them. For instance,

"The Dance of the Willow Tree" teaches us the importance of flexibility and adaptability in the face of change. Just as the willow tree bends with the wind without breaking, we too can learn to accept and adapt to life's changes gracefully. This mirrors the Buddhist teaching that resisting change only leads to suffering, while acceptance brings peace.

Similarly, "The Unyielding Stone and the Gentle Stream" illustrates the transformative power of acceptance, showing how even the hardest stone can be shaped by the gentle, persistent flow of water.

Taoism: Flowing with Change

Taoism emphasizes the importance of living in harmony with the Tao, the natural flow of the universe. The Taoist philosophy teaches that resistance to change disrupts this harmony and leads to discord. Change is seen as a natural and necessary part of life, and Taoist philosophy encourages us to move with the flow rather than resist it. By aligning ourselves with the Tao, we can navigate change with grace and ease.

"The Tale of the Blossom and the Breeze" tells of a character who learns to accept the changes brought by the seasons, finding beauty and wisdom in each phase of life. This story reflects the Taoist ideal that true harmony comes from embracing change as a natural part of the Tao.

In "The Meeting of Flow and Solidity," characters discover that balance and adaptability are key to thriving amidst life's changes, embodying the Taoist principle of flexibility and harmony.

"The Transient Garden": The garden, constantly changing with the seasons, serves as a metaphor for the impermanence of life. The characters' acceptance of the garden's changes reflects the Taoist teaching that embracing the natural flow of life leads to tranquility and contentment.

Ikigai: Purpose Through Transformation

Ikigai, the Japanese approach to finding life's true essence, integrates the idea that change can lead to growth and fulfillment. It suggests that by embracing change and finding purpose in every transformation, we can live a more meaningful and impactful life.

In "The Flowing River of Change," a character finds their Ikigai by adapting to new circumstances and discovering new opportunities for growth. This narrative aligns with the

Ikigai principle that purposeful actions, even in the face of change, lead to a fulfilling life. Similarly, "The Dance of the Everchanging Leaf" depicts a protagonist who finds joy and purpose in the continual process of transformation, demonstrating that living with purpose and adaptability leads to a meaningful and resilient life.

"The Loom of Time": The characters in this tale learn that life is like a loom, constantly weaving new patterns. By accepting the ever-changing nature of the tapestry of life, they find peace and purpose. This reflects the Ikigai principle that embracing change allows us to align our actions with our true calling.

"The Seasons of Serenity": This story emphasizes the importance of aligning one's actions with the natural rhythms of life. The characters learn that each season brings its own opportunities and challenges, and by accepting these changes, they can find serenity and purpose. This aligns with the Ikigai teaching that true fulfillment comes from adapting to life's changes and staying true to one's purpose.

THE DANCE OF THE WILLOW TREE

In a land of perpetually shifting sands and ethereal winds, a solitary willow tree named Yumiko stretched her branches beside a crystalline stream. Yumiko prided herself on her ability to remain unchanged, her roots deeply intertwined with the earth, her leaves whispering the ancient tales of the winds. The villagers revered her, finding solace beneath her sprawling canopy and witnessing the enduring wisdom and timeless beauty she symbolized.

However, the winds of time, always in motion, whispered stories of change, of lands unseen and worlds unknown. These whispers filled Yumiko with a silent, yearning curiosity, a subtle dance of thoughts contemplating the essence of existence and the inevitable nature of transformation. "Is change truly the essence of life? Is my steadfastness a denial of life's true rhythm?" Yumiko wondered.

One day, a gentle breeze, unlike any other, caressed Yumiko's leaves, singing harmonies of unseen worlds, of mountains moving and rivers changing their course. "Do not resist the dance of existence. Embrace the eternal rhythm of transformation," the breeze whispered. This subtle whisper ignited a flame within Yumiko, a desire to understand the myriad forms of existence and to experience the infinite dance of transformation.

With a deep, resounding sigh, Yumiko released her grip on the earth, allowing her spirit to glide with the winds, to dance with the sands, to merge with the waters. She witnessed the mountain's slow dance, the river's fluid transformation, and the sand's eternal drift. She felt the pain of the wilted flower and the joy of the blooming bud. She was the moon, the stars, the sun, experiencing the boundless expressions of existence.

However, this journey was not without its sorrows. Yumiko experienced the transient nature of existence, the fleeting moments of joy, and the inevitable decay of all that is. She saw the lands ravaged by time, the mountains reduced to pebbles, and the rivers lost in the boundless ocean.

Yet, within this dance of creation and destruction, Yumiko discovered a profound beauty, a harmonious rhythm, and an acceptance of the eternal cycle of change. She understood that her resistance to change was a denial of her true nature, a refusal to partake in the boundless dance of existence.

As Yumiko embraced this realization, her spirit merged with the winds, the waters, the sands, becoming a whisper, a gentle breeze, singing the harmonious melody of acceptance, of transformation, of the eternal dance of existence.

Conclusion:

The journey of Yumiko, the willow tree, serves as a profound metaphor for the acceptance of change, the embracing of transformation, and the understanding of the transient nature of existence. By releasing her resistance to change, Yumiko discovered the boundless beauty and harmonious rhythm inherent in the eternal dance of life and death. The story invites us to reflect upon our own resistance to change, to embrace the infinite expressions of existence, and to find peace in the understanding that change is the essence of life. It encourages us to release our rigid hold on our perceived identity and to harmoniously merge with the flowing rhythm of the universe, discovering the profound beauty in the acceptance of change.

THE UNYIELDING STONE AND THE GENTLE STREAM

In a secluded valley, nestled between two great mountains, flowed a serene stream named Suyin. Beside Suyin stood an ancient stone, Kaito, renowned for its unwavering presence. Suyin's waters caressed Kaito daily, and over time, the two became great companions.

Kaito took immense pride in his solidity, often boasting, "While everything around me changes, I remain the same, timeless and unyielding." He saw the world change, seasons come and go, and yet, in his perspective, he stood unaltered.

Suyin, with her gentle and flowing nature, responded, "Dear Kaito, change is the essence of existence. Even the mightiest mountains erode, and the deepest oceans shift. Do not become so entrenched in the notion of permanence."

Kaito chuckled, "You are but water, ever-changing and formless. I am the very definition of constancy."

One season, a great storm descended upon the valley. Torrential rains and fierce winds wreaked havoc. When the storm subsided, the landscape of the valley had transformed. Suyin's course had altered slightly, but Kaito believed he remained unchanged. However, to his surprise, he noticed a tiny indentation on his surface where Suyin's waters touched him.

Years turned to decades, and decades to centuries. With each passing moment, the gentle waters of Suyin caressed the stone, and the once minuscule indentation grew deeper, shaping a smooth curve on Kaito's surface.

Kaito, feeling the change within himself, lamented, "I, who prided myself on my constancy, am now marked by change. Does this mean I have lost?"

Suyin, with her boundless wisdom, whispered, "No, dear Kaito. You have merely come to understand the nature of existence. Everything undergoes transformation. The change does not diminish your essence; it simply reveals the myriad forms of beauty within you."

Kaito pondered Suyin's words deeply. Over time, he came to embrace the changes that life brought, understanding that permanence was but an illusion. He realized that the essence of existence was not in resisting change but in accepting and flowing with it.

Conclusion:

Kaito's journey from resistance to acceptance symbolizes our inherent struggle with the impermanent nature of existence. Many of us cling to the illusion of constancy, fearing change and believing that stability defines our worth. However, like Kaito, it is only through embracing the changes that we truly understand the profound beauty of life's ever-evolving dance. The tale encourages introspection on our resistance to life's natural flow and prompts us to ask: Are we, like Kaito, resisting the inevitable, or can we learn, as he did, to embrace the transformative beauty of change?

THE TALE OF THE BLOSSOM AND THE BREEZE

In a quiet village surrounded by dense forests and gentle hills, there stood a magnificent cherry blossom tree called Aleria. With each spring, Aleria would bloom in full splendor, showering the village with a canopy of pink petals.

Near Aleria, the playful breeze named Elwin danced through the village, bringing tales from distant lands. Whenever Elwin caressed Aleria, petals would detach and glide gracefully to the ground, creating a cascade of fleeting beauty.

One spring, Aleria voiced a lament, "Dear Elwin, every year I blossom with all my might, and every year you take my petals away. Why must you constantly bring about this change?"

Elwin replied with a gentle whisper, "Dearest Aleria, it's not I who takes away but the nature of life that demands movement. Your petals fall, yet they become part of the earth, nourishing it, ensuring the cycle of life continues."

Aleria, though understanding, still held reservations. "But I cherish my blossoms. They are the culmination of a year's labor. Can there not be permanence in their beauty?"

Elwin, with his ageless wisdom, answered, "The beauty of the world lies not in permanence but in the acceptance of every moment's unique splendor. Your petals, though short-lived, leave an indelible mark on the hearts of those who witness their descent. In their transience lies a message - that change, though inevitable, can be a source of profound beauty."

Years flowed like a river, and with each passing spring, Aleria bloomed, and Elwin played his part. Aleria gradually began to see the wisdom in Elwin's words. She realized that her resistance to change had prevented her from seeing the broader tapestry of life. Each fallen petal was not an end but a transition, a dance between the past and the promise of the future.

As Aleria's perception transformed, she not only embraced the changing seasons but also celebrated them. The village, too, began to observe not just the beauty of the blossoms but the grace of each falling petal, understanding the profound message it carried.

Conclusion:

Aleria's journey from resistance to celebration encapsulates the human experience of change. Our inherent desire for permanence often blinds us to the beauty inherent in transience. Through the dance of the blossom and the breeze, we are reminded that acceptance is not a passive resignation to fate but a conscious choice to see the world with eyes unclouded by preconceptions. In understanding and embracing the constant ebb and flow of life, we find not only peace but a deeper appreciation for each fleeting moment.

THE MEETING OF FLOW AND SOLIDITY

In the heart of a pristine valley flowed a serene river named Suyana. For countless cycles of the sun and moon, she meandered through the lands, nurturing them with her waters. Parallel to her banks, there rested a stone named Bhava, steadfast and unmoving. With every monsoon, when Suyana swelled in vigor, she would touch Bhava, whispering tales of the landscapes she had embraced.

One day, Suyana asked, "Bhava, have you ever pondered venturing beyond this place, experiencing the vastness of the world?"

Bhava responded, "My essence is to remain unwavering. I am content in my stillness. Yet, I often wonder about you, Suyana. Why do you ceaselessly flow, altering your path, accepting the changes the lands impose upon you?"

Suyana murmured, "Change is my nature, just as stillness is yours. As I journey, I encounter rocks, trees, and terrains of all kinds. While some paths are easy, others require me to reshape, to forge anew. This perpetual dance with change is what keeps my spirit alive, for in each adaptation, I uncover a deeper understanding of existence."

The seasons continued their rhythmic dance, and the conversations between Suyana and Bhava deepened. One day, Bhava shared a quiet revelation, "I envy your courage, Suyana. While I have remained rooted in my beliefs and patterns, you've embraced the essence of transformation."

Suyana gently replied, "Dear Bhava, there's no valor greater than that of acceptance. While I flow and embrace change, you epitomize the power of presence. Our paths are different, yet they lead to the same truth."

As years turned into centuries, an observable transformation occurred. Bhava, with his grounded presence, began to have gentle curves from Suyana's constant touch. It became evident that even in his stillness, change was inevitable.

The villagers who frequented the riverbanks began to understand the profound lesson the duo offered. Suyana and Bhava, in their unique ways, conveyed that whether one chooses to flow with life's alterations or stand resolute against them, change remains the only constant. The act of accepting this reality without resistance opened the door to wisdom.

Conclusion:

In the dance of life, where moments of stillness meet waves of change, lies the essence of existence. Suyana's fluid journey and Bhava's unwavering stance teach us that resisting life's natural flow can limit our experiences. To truly live is to embrace each twist and turn, understanding that the opportunity for growth and enlightenment lies in change. Though seemingly contrasting, the river and the stone converge to reveal the same truth: acceptance of change is not merely an act but an expansive journey into the heart of life itself.

THE FLOWING RIVER OF CHANGE

In a verdant valley nourished by the mighty Himalayas, a village prospered alongside the bank of a serene river. This river had flowed the same course for as long as the villagers could remember, providing them with fresh water and abundant fish. Its tranquil waters were a symbol of constancy and reliability.

One day, a young villager named Anaya, known for her adventurous spirit, returned to the village after spending several months traveling distant lands. She brought with her tales of vast oceans and ever-shifting dunes. Yet, amidst these tales, she whispered of a looming storm that would change the course of their beloved river.

The villagers dismissed her warnings. "The river has flowed thus for generations," they argued, "Why would it change now?"

Seasons passed, and Anaya's warning soon faded into the realm of folklore. But one fateful evening, dark clouds gathered, and a torrential downpour ensued. The river's calm waters soon turned tumultuous, and by dawn, it had carved a new path, sparing the village but changing its course forever.

Chaos ensued. The villagers lamented the loss of their old river. Their boats lay stranded, their nets were of no use, and the songs they sang of the river's old course sounded melancholic.

Seeing the sorrow her people were engulfed in, Anaya approached the village's center. "Change," she began, "is the only constant in life. Just as I witnessed oceans that roared and dunes that shifted, our river, too, has embraced a new journey. Instead of mourning what was, let us embrace what is. The river has merely taken a new path, but its essence remains unchanged. Let us adapt, just as the river has."

Many villagers resisted, holding onto the past. But a few heeded Anaya's words. They explored the new course, set their nets in different places, and soon, fish were abundant once more. The adaptable villagers prospered, while those clinging to the old ways faced hardships.

Conclusion:
Just like the river, life's course is ever-changing. Those who accept and adapt to change flourish. While it's natural to cherish memories and traditions, clinging to them at the expense of the present only

leads to suffering. In the heart of change lies an opportunity, waiting for those willing to accept and adapt. Embracing the flow of life, much like the flowing river, is the essence of true wisdom.

THE DANCE OF THE EVERCHANGING LEAF

In a secluded hamlet, nestled between the whispering mountains and whispering winds, lived people who found solace in the predictability of their days. A grand, ancient tree shaded the village, its branches a sprawling sanctuary for countless birds and its roots delving deep into the nourishing earth. This majestic tree was as old as the winds and had seen the dance of many suns and moons.

One day, a wise wanderer named Jalen, known for his profound understanding of the universe's rhythms, visited the hamlet. He carried stories of lands where mountains moved and skies changed colors. More importantly, he spoke of a prophecy – a great wind that would come and alter the grand tree's destiny forever.

The villagers, anchored in their ways, scoffed at Jalen's words. "Our tree has seen the dance of time and stood firm; why would it sway to the whims of the winds now?"

Time rolled on, and Jalen's prophecy became a shadow of a forgotten whisper. Until one day, the predicted winds arrived, singing songs of transformation, and the grand tree, for the first time, swayed in the dance of change, shedding its leaves in a whirlwind of gold and crimson.

The villagers were enveloped in a cacophony of despair. Their anchor had shifted, and the eternal had changed. The symphony of leaves now had a different tune, and their hearts ached for the days of old.

Observing the suffering, Jalen spoke to the grieving villagers with eyes as calm as the moonlit night, "Change is the eternal dance of the universe. The grand tree has embraced a new rhythm, its essence untouched by the shifting dance. Let us learn the new steps of this eternal dance and find harmony within it rather than mourn the known steps."

Many resisted, their hearts entangled in the strings of yesterday. However, some listened, learning the new dance of the winds, discovering the beauty in the everchanging symphony of leaves. These villagers found new paths and new tunes, and their lives were richer for it, while those who clung to the old rhythms found only sorrow.

Conclusion:

Life, like the grand tree, is in a constant dance with change. Acceptance and adaptation to the new rhythms bring prosperity and harmony, while resistance brings pain. Memories are precious, but when they chain the soul to the past, they hinder the dance with the present and the future. In the heart of every change, there is a hidden symphony, a hidden dance, waiting to be discovered by those willing to listen, to learn, and to adapt. To live in harmony with the universe is to embrace its everchanging dance.

THE TRANSIENT GARDEN

In the heart of a land untouched by time, there existed a tranquil garden carefully tended to by the inhabitants of a small commune. This garden was a living testament to their diligence, love, and unity. Each bloom, every shade of green, was a story of their ancestors, a legacy they vowed to preserve.

Among them lived Karunaratana, an old gardener with hands that remembered the feel of every seed they had ever sowed. His heart carried the songs of blooms past, and his soul resonated with the rhythms of the earth. But, unlike others, Karunaratana was aware of a truth many turned a blind eye to – the nature of impermanence.

One morning, as the village awoke to the songs of birds and the caress of the morning sun, they were met with a sight that drew collective gasps. The garden, overnight, had transformed.

Blooms they had known all their lives had withered, replaced by unfamiliar buds and shades of green they had never seen. The commune was swept with sorrow. Their anchor, their history, seemed to be rewriting itself, and they felt lost in their own homeland. Desperate for answers, they turned to Karunaratana, who had always shown an understanding beyond their own.

Karunaratana, looking over the changed garden with a gentle smile on his lips, addressed the anxious crowd, "What you see is the dance of life. Our garden was never meant to be static; it was never meant to be a painting frozen in time. It is a living, breathing entity, just like us. We, too, change with every breath, with every thought. And just as we embrace our growth, our evolution, we must welcome the gardens."

The villagers listened, but many found it hard to accept. Their attachment to what was made the embrace of what is challenging. But some, inspired by Karunaratana's wisdom, began to tend to the new plants, learning their stories and weaving them into the fabric of the commune's history.

Conclusion:

Life, in its essence, is change. It thrives on transformation, on evolution. While memories and legacies are sacred, they should not become chains that bind us to the past, blinding us to the beauty of the present. By embracing change, we do not forsake our history; instead, we enrich it, allowing it to breathe, grow, and inspire future generations. For in the heart of acceptance, we find peace, growth, and the true essence of life.

THE LOOM OF TIME

In a village nestled between the horizon and the heartbeats of its dwellers, there was a famed loom. This wasn't just any loom; it was believed to weave the tapestry of time itself. Centuries-old, its threads held the dreams, hopes, and memories of every villager. Its patterns were familiar, comforting, an heirloom passed down generations.

Veda, a young woman with eyes reflecting the wisdom of stars and curiosity unbounded, was the village's chosen weaver. With every new day, she continued the patterns set by her predecessors, ensuring continuity and tradition. The village took pride in the unchanging, ever-consistent tapestry.

One fateful day, a tempest raged, and when the skies cleared, Veda found that the familiar threads had been blown away, leaving behind an array of colors and textures previously unknown. The village was in turmoil. Their cherished tapestry, a testament to their shared history, seemed threatened. The idea of weaving with unfamiliar threads was inconceivable.

With a heavy heart but an undeterred spirit, Veda approached the loom. Her fingers, trembling initially, began to weave. The patterns were new, the rhythm unfamiliar. Days turned into nights, nights into days, and slowly, the tapestry began to take shape. The new threads interwove with the old, creating a tapestry that was both reminiscent of the past and hopeful for the future.

When the villagers saw the renewed tapestry, they were taken aback. The vibrant new patterns seemed to dance, telling tales of resilience, adaptation, and the beauty of the unforeseen. Some resisted, yearning for the old, while others saw the possibilities the new threads brought.

Veda, looking upon her creation, spoke to her people, "Change is an inevitable weave in the fabric of time. Our strength lies not in resisting it but in embracing it. In intertwining the old with the new, we honor our past, accept the present, and dream for the future."

Conclusion:

Life's essence lies in its ever-evolving nature. While the tapestries of our existence are woven with memories and traditions, they are also punctuated with changes, unexpected turns, and new horizons. Acceptance of change is not a departure from the past but a bridge to a richer, more diverse future. Embracing this truth allows us to craft a life filled with depth, understanding, and harmony that resonates with the universe's eternal dance.

THE SEASONS OF SERENITY

In a verdant valley cradled between two great mountains lay the village of Nirbhaynath. The people of Nirbhaynath lived in accordance with nature, harmoniously marking their time by the cycles of the seasons. Each season was met with a traditional festival celebrating its unique gifts.

The most cherished of these celebrations was the Festival of Blossoms, welcoming spring. The cherry blossom trees lining the heart of Nirbhaynath would erupt in a riot of pinks and whites, their petals painting the very air with fragrance.

As years flowed by, something unusual began to manifest. The blossoms started appearing earlier, and the winters became less harsh. The familiar cadence of the seasons began to shift. Whispered worries traveled through Nirbhaynath. The Festival of Blossoms, always held on the same day, now found trees still barren or already shedding their petals.

In the midst of this change was Lila, a young woman with a penchant for questioning and understanding. Rather than mourn the loss of the predictable, she began to observe the new patterns of nature, seeking their message.

The following year, as the day of the festival neared and the blossoms were yet to appear, Lila approached the village council. She proposed a change – to hold the Festival of Blossoms not on a set day but when the trees were in full bloom, whenever that might be.

Many in the village were aghast at the idea. "It is tradition," they exclaimed. "How can we alter what has always been?"

Lila responded, "The trees and seasons are teaching us. They adapt, evolve, and find their harmony anew. Should we not learn from them? The essence of our festival is not in its date, but in its spirit – the celebration of nature's rebirth."

After much debate, the council agreed to Lila's proposal. That year, the Festival of Blossoms was unlike any other. It wasn't held on its traditional date, but it was the most vibrant, joyous, and heartfelt celebration Nirbhaynath had seen.

Conclusion:

Life is an ever-shifting tapestry woven with threads of change. To cling rigidly to the past or tradition can sometimes blind us to the evolving beauty of the present. By embracing change, we don't abandon our roots but allow them to deepen and spread in new directions. Acceptance of change is not just an acknowledgment of life's impermanence but a celebration of its infinite possibilities.

The Quest for Inner Peace

Throughout our lives, the pursuit of inner peace is a fundamental journey. Inner peace, often described as a state of mental and emotional calm, helps us navigate the chaos of life with a sense of stability and balance. It is a profound state that allows us to remain centered and composed regardless of external circumstances. Embracing inner peace can transform our lives, leading to improved well-being, relationships, and overall happiness. The philosophies of Buddhism, Taoism, and Ikigai offer valuable insights into cultivating inner peace.

Importance of Inner Peace

Inner peace is crucial for several reasons. It enhances our mental and emotional well-being by reducing stress, anxiety, and negative emotions. This tranquility allows us to handle life's challenges more effectively, promoting resilience and emotional stability. When we achieve inner peace, we can approach situations with a clear mind and a calm demeanor, leading to better decision-making and problem-solving abilities.

Moreover, inner peace fosters healthier relationships. When we are at peace with ourselves, we can interact with others more compassionately and empathetically. This state of harmony within ourselves translates to less conflict and more meaningful connections with those around us. Additionally, inner peace enables us to let go of the need for external validation, reducing dependency on others for our happiness.

From a spiritual perspective, inner peace is often linked to a deeper connection with the self and the universe. It encourages mindfulness and presence, helping us live in the moment and appreciate life's simple pleasures. This spiritual tranquility can lead to a greater sense of purpose and fulfillment, as we align our actions with our core values and beliefs.

Buddhism: The Path to Tranquility

Buddhism teaches that inner peace is achieved by overcoming desires and attachments, which are the root causes of suffering. Mindfulness and meditation are essential practices in Buddhism that help cultivate a calm and focused mind. By being present and observing our thoughts without attachment, we can achieve a state of inner tranquility.

In the stories within this chapter, characters often embark on journeys of self-discovery and mindfulness. For example, in "Ripples of Clarity," the characters learn to remain centered and composed, finding clarity through meditation and mindful living. This mirrors the Buddhist practice of meditation, where focusing on the breath and observing the mind can lead to profound inner peace. Similarly, "Beneath the Veil of the Eternal Moon" depicts characters who find peace through letting go of desires and attachments, embodying the Buddhist path to tranquility.

"The Paradox of Inner Stillness": This tale explores the idea that true stillness and peace come from within, even in the midst of external turmoil. The characters' journey to inner stillness reflects the Buddhist practice of cultivating a calm and focused mind through meditation.

Taoism: Harmony with the Tao

Taoism emphasizes living in harmony with the Tao, the fundamental principle that underlies and unifies the universe. Inner peace, according to Taoist philosophy, is found by aligning oneself with the natural flow of life and embracing simplicity. Taoism encourages practices such as meditation, tai chi, and spending time in nature to cultivate a serene and balanced state of mind.

"The Melody of Unheard Strings" exemplifies this Taoist principle. Characters in the story learn to harmonize their actions with the natural world, finding peace in their connection to nature. This reflects the Taoist idea that inner peace comes from living in harmony with the natural world and aligning with life's ebb and flow. In "Journey to the Heart's Silent Chamber," characters discover that inner stillness and balance are key to achieving peace, embodying the Taoist principle of harmony and simplicity.

"Whispers of the Bamboo Grove": This illustrates the Taoist principle of wu wei, or effortless action. By moving with the natural flow and not against it, the characters find peace and balance, embodying the Taoist approach to life that minimizes struggle and embraces harmony.

"Silence Beyond the Murmurs": This highlights the Taoist practice of finding peace in silence and simplicity. The characters learn that true tranquility comes from quieting the mind and living simply, free from the distractions of modern life.

Ikigai: Purpose and Peace

Ikigai, the delicate Japanese art of finding one's core essence, elegantly merges the pursuit of meaning with the tranquility of inner peace. When we engage in activities that align with our passions, talents, and the needs of the world, we find a deep sense of satisfaction and tranquility. Ikigai encourages us to pursue what we love and excel at, fostering a state of inner harmony.

In "The Symphony of Unseen Breezes," a character finds their Ikigai through embracing their unique talents and contributing to their community. This narrative demonstrates that living with purpose and passion can lead to inner peace, as we align our actions with our true calling and make a positive impact on the world. Similarly, "Beneath the Veil of Illusions" explores the idea that letting go of superficial desires and focusing on meaningful actions leads to a deeper sense of peace and satisfaction. The characters learn that true happiness comes from within, aligned with their Ikigai.

RIPPLES OF CLARITY

In the dense tapestry of human existence, nestled between the peaks of desires and the valleys of despair, lay a village named Kshana. Time seemed to dance gracefully in Kshana, where every moment was a delicate balance between movement and stillness.

Among its denizens was Nibbanash, a humble seeker known not for his eloquence but for his profound silences. While the village buzzed with activity, quests for riches, and the pursuits of pleasure, Nibbanash's journey was inward. The depths of his introspections were a mystery to many, and his quest became the subject of whispered tales.

One day, as the sun painted the sky in hues of gold and crimson, a traveler from distant lands arrived, his heart heavy with burdens and his mind clouded with unrest. He had heard tales of Nibbanash and sought his wisdom.

Finding Nibbanash in his tranquil garden, meditating beside a serene pond, the traveler implored, "O wise one, I journey across lands, seeking peace which eludes me like a mirage. How does one find the oasis of inner serenity?"

Opening his eyes, Nibbanash invited the traveler to sit beside him. He then picked up a handful of the turbid water from the pond and placed it in a clear bowl. "Watch," he whispered.

As moments turned into minutes, the mud settled, and the water became clear. Nibbanash spoke softly, "Your mind, traveler, is like this water. Agitated by constant wants, fears, and memories, it remains turbid. But when left undisturbed, when given time to breathe and be, clarity emerges."

"But how does one still the constant waves of thoughts and desires?" the traveler asked.

Nibbanash smiled gently, "Not by force, for resistance only adds to the turmoil. Instead, become an observer. Let thoughts flow, but don't become entangled. Like leaves on a river, they come and they go. Find your anchor in the breath, in the present moment. For in that presence, peace blossoms."

Touched by the profound simplicity of Nibbanash's words, the traveler spent days in Kshana. With patience and practice, he began to glimpse the tranquility he sought.

Conclusion:

True peace isn't an external treasure to be found but an inner sanctuary to be cultivated. It isn't the absence of challenges but the presence of awareness. As the world continues its dance of chaos and clamor, the path to serenity lies in understanding that stillness is not devoid of movement but is a harmonious rhythm of its own. In embracing this truth, one not only observes life but truly lives.

BENEATH THE VEIL OF THE ETERNAL MOON

In a realm where the fabric of time interweaved with the threads of reality, a town named Dhvani existed. Its inhabitants were ensnared in the hustle of existence, with hearts echoing with yearnings and minds tangled in a web of thoughts.

Amidst the labyrinth of Dhvani's streets was an enigmatic woman named Aadhya. Known not for her words but for the profound calm that seemed to radiate from her very being, she was a living paradox in this bustling town.

One day, under the silvery gaze of the twilight moon, a scholar named Vihan approached her dwelling, driven by an insatiable quest for inner peace. With scrolls from countless lands and tales of many sages tucked under his arm, he beseeched Aadhya, "O beacon of stillness, I have scoured the scriptures and trodden many lands. Yet, inner peace eludes me like a fleeting shadow. Guide me."

Aadhya, looking into the depths of Vihan's seeking eyes, pointed towards the ever-present moon overhead and said, "Tell me, scholar, why does the moon shine?"

Vihan pondered, "It reflects the light of the sun."

She responded, "Yet, what makes it truly mesmerizing is not just the light it reflects but the phases it embraces. New moon, crescent, or full, it remains unaltered in its essence."

Vihan, engrossed, awaited her wisdom.

"Your quest for peace," Aadhya whispered, "is akin to the moon's journey. The world is the sun, casting its myriad reflections on your being. At times, it's overwhelming brightness; other times, shadows. Yet, true peace is in realizing your unchanging essence beneath these reflections."

Vihan, struck by the realization, mused, "So, it is not about silencing the outer world, but recognizing the silence within?"

Aadhya nodded, "True inner peace isn't an escape from reality, but a deeper understanding of it. Embrace the phases, yet remain rooted in your innate tranquility."

Conclusion:

The pursuit of inner peace is not an external journey but an inward realization. Just as the moon retains its essence regardless of its phases, so too does our inner being remain constant amidst life's fluctuations. The key lies not in seeking a silent realm but in attuning to the silent space within, where peace isn't a quest but a timeless truth.

THE MELODY OF UNHEARD STRINGS

In a land that was timeless, bathed in perpetual twilight, lay a city named Sunyatamuni. Its winding alleys were filled with the symphony of life: joy, sorrow, ambitions, and regrets.

In Sunyatamuni's heart was a revered grove, and in its center stood an ancient lyre, untouched and unplayed, yet said to hold the universe's melody. Its strings were not visible to the eye, and its music was unheard by the ear.

One day, a seeker named Chara, with turmoil in her heart and shadows in her mind, arrived in Sunyatamuni. She had heard of the lyre and believed its melody would offer her the inner peace she desperately sought.

Upon reaching the grove, she gazed at the lyre, her heart swelling with anticipation. But hours turned to days, and she neither saw its strings nor heard its song. Frustration grew as the silent lyre mirrored her internal chaos.

An old sage, having observed her persistent efforts, approached. "What do you seek from the lyre, young traveler?"

"The song of inner peace," Chara responded, her voice tinged with despair.

The sage, looking deeply into the horizon, began, "Do you hear the rustling leaves, the chirping crickets, or the distant waterfall?"

"Yes," Chara replied, "I hear them all."

"The lyre's song," the sage continued, "is not in its strings or its melody but in the silence between the sounds. It's in the pauses, the stillness, the unplayed notes. That is where true peace lies."

Chara closed her eyes, focusing not on the sounds but the spaces in between. Slowly, the cacophony of her inner world faded, and in its place emerged a serene stillness, a melody of peace she had yearned for.

Conclusion:
The world resonates with myriad sounds and distractions, but true inner peace is found not in the noise but in the silence between. It isn't about hearing a particular song but tuning into the spaces, the unsaid, the untouched. Like the unheard strings of a lyre, it's the intangible moments of stillness that hold the most profound truths. Seeking peace is less about finding a melody and more about understanding the silence.

JOURNEY TO THE HEART'S SILENT CHAMBER

The Kingdom of Antardhwani was nestled between the mountains, caressed by the serene touch of wind and sun. It was famous, not for its wealth or might, but for a unique temple called The Hall of Echoes. Pilgrims from distant lands were drawn to its enigma. They said the temple could reflect the true sound of one's soul.

Amaya, a bright-eyed wanderer from a far-off land, was on a quest to find inner peace. She had sailed the seven seas, scaled the highest peaks, and walked through endless deserts in search of tranquility. Upon hearing about The Hall of Echoes, she felt a magnetic pull and began her pilgrimage to Antardhwani.

When she finally stood at the entrance of the temple, she took a deep breath and stepped inside. The vast hall was silent, with walls adorned in crystalline patterns. She walked to the center, whispered her deepest desire, "Peace," and waited for the hall to echo her soul's sound.

To her surprise, she was met with a cacophony of voices — voices of her past regrets, unmet desires, anxieties, and pains. Distraught, she sank to her knees, feeling more lost than ever.

Just then, an elderly monk, the guardian of the temple, approached. With compassionate eyes, he said, "Dear seeker, why do you grieve?"

Tears streaming down, Amaya replied, "I came seeking peace, but all I found was chaos within."

The monk gently responded, "The Hall of Echoes only amplifies what's already there. It doesn't judge or alter. To find peace, you must first acknowledge the dissonance within."

Amaya pondered on his words and asked, "How can I find the peace I seek?"

The monk, pointing towards her heart, answered, "The journey to peace doesn't lie in silencing the noise outside but in harmonizing the sounds within. Sit, close your eyes, and listen, not with the intent to answer but with the will to understand."

With newfound clarity, Amaya meditated, delving deep into her inner world, listening, understanding, and embracing every sound of her soul. As days turned into weeks, the chaos slowly transmuted into a harmonious symphony, resonating with the true sound of inner peace.

Conclusion:

Peace isn't an external treasure to be found but an inner state to be cultivated. The quest for inner tranquility is less about escaping the noise and more about understanding and harmonizing the dissonance within. It reminds us that, in the orchestration of life, every note, be it joy or sorrow, has its place in the creation of our soul's unique melody.

THE SYMPHONY OF UNSEEN BREEZES

In the tapestry of realms existed a domain known as Manas, a place cloaked in wisdom's essence and the musings of the cosmos. In this abode of enlightenment, a silent lake called The Mirror of Tranquility resided, which was said to reflect the truth of one's inner essence.

A wise yet troubled soul, Jetsunma found herself at the shores of Manas, her heart heavy with the unseen weights of life. She sought the tranquility and inner silence that seemed like a forgotten whisper in the winds.

Approaching the Mirror of Tranquility, she peered into its depth, hoping to find the serene reflections of her essence. Instead, she witnessed the turbulent waves of her unspoken fears, unheard cries, and unfulfilled longings.

Disheartened, she sat beside the lake, her thoughts a storm in the silent realm. It was then that a guardian of Manas, an old, serene sage, appeared beside her, his presence a symphony of unseen breezes.

"Why does my reflection show turbulence when I seek tranquility?" Jetsunma asked, her voice a quiver in the eternal silence.

"The mirror," the sage whispered, "only reveals what resides within. To see tranquility, one must become tranquility."

"But how?" Jetsunma implored, her eyes wells of untold stories.

"Close your eyes," the sage guided, "and listen to the whispers of your soul, embrace the unseen breezes of your essence, dance with the shadows and the lights within."

Jetsunma, her heart open and mind still, immersed in her inner symphony, felt every note of her being, the pain, the joy, the love, the loss. She embraced them all, not as fragments but as harmonious parts of her whole self.

As she danced in her inner winds, the turbulent waves in the mirror calmed, reflecting a tranquility more profound than the silent realms of Manas.

Conclusion:
The Symphony of Unseen Breezes unfolds the truth that peace isn't a destination but a state of being. To witness tranquility within, one must dance with every unseen breeze of their essence. True inner peace is found when one embraces every part of their being and sees

the harmony in their internal symphony. It challenges us not to seek peace in the external world but to cultivate it within, to become a silent realm of our own, reflecting the profound tranquility of our harmonized essence.

BENEATH THE VEIL OF ILLUSIONS

In a city where the din of modernity echoed and the pace was relentless lived Lhundup, a woman of grace and wisdom but cloaked in the worldly garbs of anxiety. Skyscrapers seemed to touch the heavens, but the souls below, including Lhundup's, felt earthbound, heavy with burdens.

One evening, amidst the crimson hues of sunset, Lhundup stood on her balcony, overlooking the bustling streets below. As the sun dipped beneath the horizon, she felt an echoing descent within her heart. A sense of tranquility eluded her for all her achievements, wealth, and connections. The cacophony of the world outside mirrored the tumultuous emotions within her.

That night, as sleep remained a distant dream, Lhundup made a decision. She embarked on a journey to the revered Himalayas, hearing tales of monks who possessed the knowledge to calm turbulent minds.

The rugged path was a stark contrast to the plush interiors of her city apartment. She climbed for days, each step challenging her resolve, making her question her own pursuit. Finally, at the crest of a snowy peak, she found an old monastery, its walls bearing the weight of countless winters.

A monk, his face lined with age yet eyes shining with youthful clarity, greeted her. Without uttering a word, he seemed to know her purpose. In the silent courtyard, he posed a riddle: "What remains when all is stripped away?"

For days, Lhundup pondered on this, seeking the answer in the scriptures, in meditation, and in the whispering winds. She confronted her fears, her aspirations, her memories, and her dreams.

One evening, as the soft glow of lanterns lit the courtyard, understanding dawned upon Lhundup. Approaching the monk, she whispered, "The true self."

The monk, with a knowing smile, responded, "To find peace, one must not seek it in the external world but uncover it within. It is not a destination, but a realization."

Conclusion:
Beneath the Veil of Illusions beckons us to reflect upon our incessant search for external validations, accomplishments, and distractions. It urges one to dive deep within and to question what truly remains when all superficial layers are peeled away. As Lhundup discovered, true inner peace is not found on the highest mountain or the deepest

ocean but within the silent chambers of our hearts. The journey to uncover it requires courage, introspection, and the shedding of countless veils of illusions that shroud our authentic selves. Only by embracing our inherent essence can we find the tranquility that remains steadfast amidst the ever-changing currents of life.

WHISPERS OF THE BAMBOO GROVE

In a distant village nestled between rolling hills and serene lakes, the rhythm of life was slow, and the melodies of nature echoed in every corner. Here, Lian, a young man with dreams bigger than the vast skies, felt confined by tradition and yearned for the excitement of the city.

Eager to escape, Lian moved to a sprawling metropolis. The neon lights dazzled him, the pace exhilarated him, and the plethora of choices overwhelmed him. He thrived, building a successful life replete with luxuries. Yet, as the years rolled on, a gnawing emptiness began to shadow him.

The silence of the night brought with it a deafening noise of his inner conflicts. His success felt shallow, his relationships transient. The peace he once took for granted in his village now seemed like a distant memory.

Desperate to reclaim that serenity, Lian visited therapists, attended workshops, and even took sabbaticals to exotic destinations, seeking answers. Yet, the turmoil only intensified.

One evening, a chance encounter with an old sage at a park bench shifted his perspective. The sage, sensing Lian's distress, pointed towards a bamboo grove swaying gracefully to the city's cacophony.

"See those bamboos?" he said, "They thrive amidst this chaos, not by resisting it, but by dancing with it."

Lian looked on, intrigued.

The sage continued, "Inner peace is not an escape from our challenges but a deep understanding and acceptance of them. It's about finding harmony within, even when the world outside is in disarray."

Lian spent hours, then days, sitting by the bamboo grove, absorbing its quiet wisdom. He realized that he had been seeking peace in places and people, treating it as a destination. All along, it was a state of being waiting to be discovered within him.

Embracing this revelation, Lian's approach to life transformed. He no longer saw the city's noise as a disturbance but as a melody, he could harmonize with. His relationships deepened, his work gained purpose, and the void that once haunted him was replaced with a contented tranquility.

Conclusion:

Whispers of the Bamboo Grove nudges us to reconsider our external quests for peace. The relentless pursuit of tranquility outside often distracts us from the sanctuary of calm within. Just like the bamboo, resilient yet flexible, we too can find our rhythm amidst life's chaos. Inner peace is less about changing our surroundings and more about reshaping our inner perspective. By finding that harmonious balance, we can navigate life's complexities not with resistance but with grace and acceptance.

THE PARADOX OF INNER STILLNESS

In a secluded monastery perched upon a misty mountain, monks draped in saffron robes practiced diligent meditation. Among them was Laksh, a monk known for his profound stillness. To many, it appeared as though Laksh had already attained the coveted inner peace, they all sought. But deep inside, a tempestuous storm raged.

Laksh's mind was like a turbulent river, memories of past regrets, fears of future uncertainties, and a constant yearning to achieve a state of true inner calm. Though he sat with an enviable serenity, his internal world was in disarray.

One day, a venerable old monk, Ratnashri, approached Laksh. Without a word being spoken, Ratnashri discerned the battle within Laksh's soul. "Come with me," he beckoned.

They ventured outside the monastery, walking silently until they reached a pristine lake, its waters reflecting the cerulean sky above. Throwing a stone into the lake, Ratnashri gestured to Laksh to observe the ripples.

"The quest for inner peace," began Ratnashri, "is much like these ripples. When we force or chase it, we create disturbances. But with patience, every ripple, every thought, every emotion settles, revealing the clarity beneath."

Laksh contemplated deeply on this. Realizing he had been clinging to the idea of peace, he had inadvertently moved further from it.

In the days that followed, Laksh no longer strived for calm but simply observed his emotions and thoughts, letting them flow like water down a stream, without attachment, without judgment.

Gradually, the turbulent river of his mind began to still, not because he sought stillness but because he allowed the natural course of things. He learned that true inner peace wasn't an achievement but a realization. It was not in the absence of storms but in understanding and embracing them.

Conclusion:
The tale of Laksh reminds us that in our zealous quest for peace, we often become the creators of our own unrest. True peace is not to be chased but realized. It is not about silencing our storms but understanding them. When we stop trying to control and start

observing with compassion and detachment, we discover that the depth of still waters has always been present beneath the tumultuous waves.

SILENCE BEYOND THE MURMURS

In a village nestled between mountains that touched the heavens, there resided Tarun, a man praised for his wisdom yet tormented by an unquenchable thirst for inner tranquility. He felt the weight of his inner chaos, a cacophony that contrasted starkly against the serenity of his environment.

One day, as Tarun wandered through the village, he chanced upon a blind artist, Vishala, sculpting with profound concentration. Each stroke she made was imbued with grace and certainty as if she could see beyond the veil of the visible. Struck by the paradox of her situation, Tarun posed a question, "Vishala, in a world shrouded in darkness for you, how do you sculpt with such precision and peace?"

Vishala, pausing her hands for a moment, responded, "Tarun, the world isn't dark for me; it's just different. I've learned not to search for the light but to find beauty and peace within the darkness."

Sensing an underlying wisdom, Tarun sat beside her, "Please, tell me more."

"The world around us," she began, "is filled with externalities that can either be a source of endless distraction or profound realization. I do not see the sun rise or set, but I feel its warmth. I can't behold the colors of the spring, but I sense its life. My world, devoid of sight, taught me to find harmony within."

Tarun meditated on her words. He realized that his search for peace was outward, in rituals, scriptures, and affirmations. But true peace, as reflected in Vishala's world, was a journey inward. It wasn't about silencing the murmurs but listening to them, understanding them, and finding the underlying silence.

Motivated by this newfound understanding, Tarun retreated to a secluded corner of the mountains. With each passing day, rather than resisting the racket inside, he listened. He embraced. He understood. Over time, the noise faded not because it was forced out but because Tarun found the silence beneath it. It was always there, just waiting to be discovered.

Conclusion:
We unearth a profound truth in Vishala's darkness and Tarun's journey. Inner peace isn't about escaping or combating the disturbances around or within us. It's about delving deeper,

understanding the nature of our turmoil, and uncovering the inherent serenity that exists beneath. Like the silent depths of an ocean beneath turbulent waves, true tranquility lies not in the absence of noise but in the discovery of the silence beyond it.

The Balance of Work and Rest

In the relentless pace of modern life, finding the balance between work and rest is crucial for maintaining our physical health, mental harmony, and overall happiness. We explore in this chapter the delicate dance between diligence and relaxation, illustrating how the philosophies of Buddhism, Taoism, and Ikigai guide us toward a harmonious life where effort and ease coexist in perfect synergy. By understanding these principles, we are encouraged to live a life of balance, where work and rest complement each other, leading to a more fulfilling existence.

Importance of Balancing Work and Rest

Finding equilibrium between work and rest is essential for maintaining overall well-being and productivity for several reasons. It enhances productivity and creativity by preventing burnout and maintaining high levels of energy and focus. Regular periods of rest and relaxation allow the mind to rejuvenate, leading to better problem-solving abilities and innovative thinking. Moreover, a balanced life reduces stress and promotes emotional stability, contributing to better mental health and overall well-being.

Work-life balance also fosters healthier relationships. When we allocate time for rest and leisure, we can engage more meaningfully with our loved ones, building stronger and more supportive connections. Additionally, this balance allows us to pursue personal interests and hobbies, enriching our lives beyond professional achievements.

From a spiritual perspective, balancing work and rest aligns us with natural rhythms and cycles, promoting a sense of harmony and inner peace. It encourages mindfulness and presence, helping us appreciate the value of each moment, whether in activity or in repose.

Buddhism: The Middle Way

Buddhism teaches the Middle Way, a path of moderation that avoids the extremes of self-indulgence and self-mortification. This philosophy highlights the significance of balance in every aspect of life, including work and rest. By practicing mindfulness and maintaining equilibrium, we can achieve inner peace and enlightenment.

In the stories within this chapter, characters often explore the concept of balance. For instance, "The Harmony of Effort and Ease" illustrates how maintaining a balanced approach to work and rest leads to a more fulfilling and productive life. This mirrors the Buddhist teaching of the Middle Way, where balance and moderation are key to achieving spiritual and personal growth.

Taoism: Harmony with the Tao

Taoism emphasizes living in harmony with the Tao, the fundamental principle that underlies and unifies the universe. This philosophy advocates for a balanced life where work and rest are in sync with the natural flow of the Tao. Taoism encourages practices such as meditation, tai chi, and spending time in nature to cultivate a serene and balanced state of mind.

"The Cosmic Dance of Duty and Dream" exemplifies this Taoist principle. Characters in the story learn to balance their responsibilities with their personal aspirations, finding peace in their daily routines. This reflects the Taoist idea that true harmony comes from aligning one's actions with the natural rhythms of life. In "Bhima's Path to Equilibrium," characters discover that balance and adaptability are key to thriving amidst life's demands, embodying the Taoist principle of harmony and simplicity.

Ikigai: Purposeful Balance

Ikigai, the ancient Japanese art of discovering one's true purpose, integrates the idea that a meaningful life includes a balance between work and rest. When we engage in activities that align with our passions, talents, and the needs of the world, we find a deep sense of satisfaction and tranquility. Ikigai encourages us to pursue what we love and excel at, fostering a state of inner harmony.

In "Weaving the Fabric of Life," a character finds their Ikigai through balancing their professional duties with personal passions, creating a fulfilling and balanced life. This narrative demonstrates that living with purpose and balance can lead to inner peace, as we align our actions with our true calling and make a positive impact on the world. Similarly, "The Tale of Two Dancers" depicts characters who find joy and purpose by balancing their work and rest, highlighting the Ikigai principle that balance leads to a meaningful and resilient life.

THE HARMONY OF EFFORT AND EASE

Once, in a village nestled between two mountains, in the realm of time unmeasured, lived a humble artisan named Devan, known for his craftsmanship and diligence. He toiled from the sun's first light till the moon took its throne, embodying the essence of ceaseless effort. However, his world was confined to the monotonous rhythm of work, leaving no space for the soothing dance of repose.

One tranquil morning, a wandering monk draped in robes of saffron entered the village. He spoke of a middle way, a harmonious blend of industrious effort and rejuvenating rest, a path leading to the most radiant realms of inner peace.

Devan, drawn to the monk's words like a moth to a flame, approached him, his heart pulsating with the echo of newfound wisdom. "Venerable One," he queried, "How does one traverse this middle path, balancing the scales of work and rest, and uncover the treasure of serene existence?"

The monk, sensing the ripeness of Devan's soul, replied with a story filled with the essence of profound truth. "Once, a musician sought to tune his sitar, pondering on the tautness of its strings. Too loose, the strings would fail to sing the symphony of existence; too tight, and they would snap, silencing the music of the spheres."

He continued, "So is the dance of life, a delicate balance between striving and surrendering, between acting and allowing. To walk the middle path, one must cultivate the wisdom to discern when to push and when to pause, when to forge ahead and when to let the river of life carry them to the shores of tranquility."

Devan, absorbing the elixir of the monk's words, began to see the world through the lens of an enlightened perspective. He learned to weave moments of stillness into the fabric of his day, to listen to the whispers of the wind and the symphony of the stars. His hands still danced with the rhythm of creation, but his soul learned the sweet taste of rest.

The fruits of this harmonious living were abundant. His creations reflected the beauty of a balanced existence, and his heart became a wellspring of joy and peace. The whole village, witnessing the transformation of Devan, embarked on the journey to embrace the middle way, filling the air with the melody of harmonious living.

Conclusion:

The parable of Devan serves as a luminous beacon, guiding us through the tumultuous seas of existence. It invites us to reflect upon our own dance of life, to question the strings of our being—are they too tight, bound by the relentless pursuit of doing, or too loose, lost in the ocean of indolence?

The middle way whispers the secret of enlightened living, inviting us to embrace both effort and ease to find harmony in the dichotomy of existence. It is the golden key to unlocking the gates of inner peace, allowing the soul to soar in the boundless skies of serene bliss. In the delicate balance between work and rest, we find the symphony of life, a melody that sings the song of the cosmos, inviting all of existence to dance in the rhythm of eternal harmony.

WEAVING THE FABRIC OF LIFE

In a village cushioned amidst the jade hills and sapphire streams resided Sherpa, a masterful weaver known far and wide. The rhythmic clack of his loom was a familiar sound from dawn to dusk. His impeccable textiles, adorned with intricate patterns, mirrored the universe's grand tapestry. But as days turned to years, Sherpa's fingers grew weary, and his spirit dimmed.

On an auspicious day, a sage with eyes deep as the cosmos journeyed into the village. Settling under the ancient Bodhi tree, he drew villagers near with tales of wisdom and enlightenment.

Curious, Sherpa approached the sage, his heart burdened with exhaustion. "Great Seer," he whispered, "I labor with unmatched dedication, but the essence of life seems to slip like sand between my fingers. How do I entwine the threads of work and rest?"

Sensing the depth of Sherpa's plight, the sage began with a gentle smile, "Imagine, dear weaver, a loom ever-working without pause. The threads would entangle, the patterns would blur, and the loom's song would become a cacophony of chaos."

He continued, "Life, like your loom, seeks rhythm — a delicate dance of effort and pause. The universe itself rests between breaths, allowing stars to shine and galaxies to turn. In your pursuit of perfection, remember that rest is not the absence of work, but the very essence that rejuvenates and brings forth brilliance."

The sage then motioned to the nearby stream, "Watch how the water flows with vigor, then finds pockets of stillness, reflecting the heavens. Embrace such moments of reflection, for they are the universe's whispers guiding your spirit."

With newfound clarity, Sherpa returned to his loom. While he wove with the same fervor, he also found moments of stillness, letting his fingers trace the patterns of the cosmos, allowing his soul to drink from the nectar of rest.

The textiles born from this new rhythm were unlike any other. They resonated with the dance of the universe, captivating all who laid eyes upon them. Sherpa's weaving became a meditation, a harmonious blend of fervor and tranquility.

Conclusion:

Sherpa's journey unveils the profound wisdom embedded in the balance of action and inaction. As seekers in this vast cosmos, it is essential to understand that the dance of life is not about perpetual motion but about finding harmony between movement and stillness. It reminds us that true mastery, true understanding, and genuine peace emanate not just from relentless work but from the sacred pauses that allow us to align with the universe's rhythm. Such balance challenges our modern conventions and beckons us to embrace a deeper, more harmonious rhythm — the eternal dance of work and rest.

BHIMA'S PATH TO EQUILIBRIUM

A gifted musician, Bhima lived in a small village nestled among the rolling hills and serenading streams. His bamboo flute's melodies resonated with emotions so profound that it seemed like the very wind took lessons from him. Each day, as the sun painted the sky with golden hues, villagers would gather around the community square, their hearts and ears attuned to Bhima's music.

One day, a monk with an air of serenity around him arrived at the village. Drawn by the flute's hauntingly beautiful notes, he approached Bhima. After the performance, the monk inquired, "Your music is a balm to the soul, but tell me, Bhima, how do you produce such heavenly sounds?"

Bhima, humbled, replied, "I pour my entire self into the music. I play from sunrise to sunset, letting my fingers dance non-stop on the bamboo."

The monk nodded, "Your dedication is evident. However, consider the flute itself, Bhima. Does it not teach us something invaluable? It is not just the played holes that produce melodies but also the silent spaces between them. Similarly, life's melody emerges not just from ceaseless activity but also from the spaces of stillness we embrace."

He continued, "The universe, in its wisdom, has given day and night, activity and rest. By denying yourself the pause, you might miss out on a richer, deeper tone that resides in the silences."

Bhima pondered upon the monk's words. The next day, he played fewer hours but listened more to the world around him — the rustling leaves, the chirping birds, and the silent whispers of the wind. He rested, reflected, and absorbed the symphony of life.

And when he played his flute again, the music was unlike before. It carried with it the depth of silence, the beauty of rest, and the wisdom of balance. The villagers, too, noticed this transformation. His melodies were no longer just tunes but stories, emotions, and the very heartbeat of the universe.

Conclusion:

Bhima's musical journey offers a profound reflection on the delicate interplay between work and rest. It challenges the ingrained belief that continuous effort is the sole path to excellence. By recognizing the wisdom inherent in pauses, silences, and rest, we not only rejuvenate our spirits but also gain a deeper understanding of our craft and life itself. Just as in music, the balance between notes and rests creates a harmonious melody; in life, it's the equilibrium between work and reprieve that crafts a meaningful existence.

THE COSMIC DANCE OF DUTY AND DREAM

Once, in a serene village set against the backdrop of undulating hills, there lived a potter named Charan. As dawn broke, he began his work every morning, molding clay with utmost precision and dedication. By noon, his shelves were adorned with exquisite pots, ready to be sold in the market.

Adjacent to Charan's workshop stood a towering banyan tree, under whose shade rested a hermit, Muditalay. Every day, he observed Charan's ceaseless efforts and the sweat that dripped from his brow. The hermit spent his days in meditation, contemplation, and occasional interactions with those seeking his wisdom.

One particularly sweltering day, Charan collapsed from exhaustion. Muditalay rushed to his aid, offering water and a cool spot beneath the banyan. Once Charan regained some strength, Muditalay softly spoke, "My friend, your diligence is unparalleled. But remember, even the mightiest rivers find their respite in tranquil lakes. Why do you push yourself so?"

Charan responded, "To provide for my family, to ensure a prosperous future. Isn't hard work the path to success?"

Muditalay nodded, "Indeed, work is essential. However, just as the day gives way to night, and the seasons change in their due time, there must be a balance. Continuous toil without rest diminishes the spirit and weakens the body."

"But how do I find this balance?" Charan asked, his eyes seeking clarity.

Muditalay gently responded, "Start by observing nature. See how the day, with all its activity, transitions to a peaceful night. Witness how the fields are left to rest after being plowed and sown, allowing crops to flourish. In the same way, interweave moments of pause and reflection into your routine. In stillness, you will find rejuvenation."

Taking Muditalay's words to heart, Charan began to change. He took breaks, meditated, and even spent time simply watching the river's gentle flow. Not only did his health improve, but the quality of his pots reached new heights. They were no longer just vessels but pieces of art, each telling a tale of balance and harmony.

Conclusion:

In our relentless quest for success and achievement, we often forget the wisdom inherent in nature's rhythm. The tale of Charan and Muditalay serves as a subtle reminder of the value of balance in our lives. Just as Charan discovered, in embracing moments of rest and reflection, we don't hinder our progress; we enhance it. By honoring both work and rest, we pave the way for true fulfillment and profound inner peace.

THE TALE OF TWO DANCERS

In the heart of the serene town of Nalanda, an old man named Sanghavir often sat under a sprawling banyan tree, playing his flute. To those who passed by, it might have seemed that Sanghavir had chosen a life of relaxation and leisure, far removed from the hardworking spirit of the town.

One sunny afternoon, a young merchant named Arav ventured near Sanghavir's usual spot, his face marked with the lines of fatigue and burden. Intrigued by the old man's calm demeanor, Arav decided to take a moment from his relentless schedule and asked, "Old man, do you not feel the weight of the world? How can you find so much time to sit and play your flute when there's work to be done?"

Sanghavir ceased his playing and looked up at Arav with twinkling eyes. "Young man, tell me, why do you work?"

"To sustain my life, to feed my family, to build my dreams," Arav replied confidently.

Sanghavir nodded. "And after working tirelessly, don't you take a moment to rest and rejuvenate?"

Arav frowned, "Rarely. The demands of life leave me little room to rest."

Sanghavir smiled gently. "Consider the sun and the moon," he began, pointing at the sky. "The sun tirelessly illuminates our world, giving us warmth and light. But even the mighty sun sets, allowing the gentle moon to take over, providing us a softer light, giving the world a moment to rest."

He continued, "Life is not just about ceaseless work. It's a balance, a dance between exertion and relaxation. The sun and moon, day and night, work and rest - they all coexist in harmony. When you neglect rest, you're disregarding the essential rhythm of life."

Arav looked contemplative. "But there's always so much to do. How can I afford to rest?"

Sanghavir chuckled softly. "And how can you afford not to? Rest doesn't take away from your work; it complements it. Just as sleep rejuvenates us for the next day, moments of calm and stillness during the day can refresh your mind and spirit."

The old man resumed playing his flute, the notes floating in the air, hinting at the delicate balance of life. Arav, feeling a newfound realization, sat down next to Sanghavir, closing his eyes and allowing the music to wash over him.

The day melted into evening, and as the first stars began to appear, Arav stood up, his face serene. "Thank you," he murmured, his voice filled with gratitude.

From that day on, Arav not only worked with more energy but also took moments to rest and reflect. And every once in a while, he would join Sanghavir under the banyan tree, learning the art of balance, the delicate dance between work and rest.

Conclusion:
The ancient wisdom found in the story of Sanghavir and Arav reminds us that life is not about constant exertion. Instead, it's about understanding the rhythm and dance of existence. Work provides sustenance and purpose, but rest rejuvenates the soul and spirit. Embracing both with grace leads to a life of harmony and fulfillment. In our modern world, where the pace is often frantic, recognizing the need for balance is not just a luxury; it's a necessity.

Forgiveness and Letting Go

Forgiveness and letting go are transformative actions that can liberate us from past burdens and pave the way for personal growth and inner peace. We delve into the power of forgiveness, illustrating how the philosophies of Buddhism, Taoism, and Ikigai guide us toward releasing anger, resentment, and guilt. By embracing these principles, we can live with greater compassion, unlocking a sense of freedom and clarity that allows us to move forward with our lives, unencumbered by the past.

Importance of Forgiveness and Letting Go

Forgiveness is essential for emotional and mental well-being. It helps release negative emotions such as anger, resentment, and bitterness, which can harm our health and happiness. Letting go of past grievances allows us to move forward with a lighter heart and a clearer mind, fostering a sense of peace and contentment.

Forgiveness has significant emotional and psychological benefits. Holding onto grudges and harboring resentment will create barriers, leading to isolation and disconnection, this also can lead to chronic stress, anxiety, and depression. These negative emotions can drain our energy, affect our mental health, and prevent us from experiencing joy and contentment. By forgiving and letting go, we release these toxic emotions, which can lead to a profound sense of relief and emotional liberation.

Forgiveness also plays a crucial role in improving our relationships. By forgiving, we open the door to reconciliation and stronger, more empathetic connections. Letting go of past grievances allows us to approach relationships with a fresh perspective, free from the baggage of old wounds. This openness can lead to more meaningful and fulfilling interactions, built on trust and mutual respect. Forgiveness transforms our relationships, enabling us to connect with others on a more genuine and compassionate level. Moreover, forgiveness is about self-forgiveness, accepting our imperfections and past mistakes, which is vital for personal growth and self-compassion.

From a spiritual perspective, forgiveness is often seen as a path to enlightenment and inner freedom. It encourages us to let go of ego-driven judgments and embrace a more compassionate and understanding outlook on life. This spiritual release can lead to a deeper sense of purpose and harmony, as we align ourselves with higher values of love and kindness.

Buddhism: The Path of Compassion

Buddhism teaches that forgiveness is essential for overcoming suffering and achieving enlightenment. By cultivating compassion and understanding, we can let go of anger and resentment, seen as obstacles to spiritual growth.

Mindfulness and meditation are key practices that help develop a forgiving heart.

In the stories within this chapter, characters embark on journeys of forgiveness and compassion. "Blossoms of the Unburdened Heart" portrays characters releasing their grievances and finding peace through compassion and understanding. This mirrors the Buddhist practice of cultivating loving-kindness (metta) and forgiveness to overcome suffering and achieve inner peace.

Taoism: Flowing with Acceptance

Taoism emphasizes living in harmony with the Tao, the natural flow of the universe. Forgiveness involves accepting the natural course of events and letting go of resistance. By aligning ourselves with the Tao, we can release negative emotions and find peace in acceptance.

"The Cavern of Grudges" exemplifies this Taoist principle. Characters learn to let go of their grudges and embrace the flow of life, finding peace in acceptance and non-resistance. This reflects the Taoist idea that true harmony comes from releasing negative emotions and living according to the natural rhythms of life. In "The Unseen Chains of Viparyaya Valley," characters discover that forgiveness and acceptance are key to achieving serenity, embodying the Taoist principle of harmony and simplicity.

Ikigai: Purposeful Release

Ikigai, highlights that forgiveness and letting go are essential for living a meaningful and impactful life. When we release negative emotions and past grievances, we create space for positive actions and purposeful living. Ikigai encourages us to focus on what truly matters, fostering a state of inner harmony.

In "The Sacred Saga of Serenity," a character finds their Ikigai through the process of forgiveness and letting go, creating a fulfilling and peaceful life. This narrative demonstrates that living with purpose and forgiveness can lead to inner peace, as we align our actions with our true calling and contribute positively to the world. The act of letting go is gratifying, as it liberates us from the burdens that hold us back. "The Weightless Pebble" illustrates how characters find joy and purpose by releasing their burdens, highlighting the Ikigai principle that forgiveness and letting go lead to a meaningful and resilient life.

THE UNSEEN ANCHOR OF ANILA

In the golden shadows of a sacred Muditalay tree, a village named Dharampura thrived, where harmony seemingly reigned supreme. But beneath the surface, hidden tales of sorrow were etched into the hearts of many, none more so than young Anila.

With her sun-kissed skin and eyes deep as the monsoon clouds, Anila was the village's cherished songbird. Yet, her voice had fallen silent ever since the betrayal of her closest confidant, Deva, who had shared her melodies with wandering minstrels for mere coins.

Hurt, she clung to her sense of betrayal, turning her back on her once-beloved craft and refusing any overtures of reconciliation from Deva.

As the years went by, Anila's pain transformed her. The vibrant songbird became a shadow, withdrawing from the joyous rhythm of village life.

One evening, an elder monk named Vishuddha, known for his profound insights, entered Dharampura. Drawn by Anila's stifled essence, he approached her. "Child, why do you carry such a heavy anchor when the vast ocean of life beckons you to sail?"

Anila, tears brimming, shared her story of betrayal. Vishuddha listened intently, then invited her to the village pond the next dawn.

There, Vishuddha handed Anila a clay pot filled with water. "Walk around the pond carrying this, but ensure not a drop spills."

Hours passed as Anila circled, her focus unwavering. When finally called to stop, her limbs ached, and exhaustion consumed her.

Vishuddha inquired, "How heavy was the pot when you began, and how heavy is it now?"

Anila pondered, "It was light initially but grew heavier with time."

The monk softly responded, "Such is the nature of resentment. Over time, what starts as a slight becomes an unbearable weight. The longer you hold onto it, the more it drains you."

Looking into the still waters of the pond, Anila saw her reflection, the weight of years visible in her gaze. She understood.

Seeking Deva, Anila extended her heart, "Deva, the silence between us has lasted too long. The melodies we once cherished are more significant than the pains of the past."

Reunited, the two created tunes that echoed the essence of forgiveness, enveloping Dharampura in a renewed harmony.

Conclusion:

Every soul, in its journey, confronts moments of pain and betrayal. Yet, it's the choice to hold onto this pain or release it that defines our path forward. Anila's tale is a gentle reminder that the anchors we carry, though unseen, hinder our true potential. By letting go, not only do we find our lost rhythm, but we also open the door for renewed melodies to grace our existence. In forgiveness, we find not just peace but also the freedom to soar higher than ever before.

BLOSSOMS OF THE UNBURDENED HEART

In the heart of a serene valley, cushioned by emerald meadows, lay the village of Niranjana. Here, the wisdom of ages whispered through the rustling leaves and the murmurs of flowing waters. Among the villagers was a woman named Mira, a diligent gardener whose flowers were not of this world; they were her emotions, carefully sowed in the inner garden of her heart.

For every emotion she acknowledged, a flower bloomed. Joy birthed vibrant lilies, love sprouted roses, and so on. However, in one corner, shadows loomed where thorny brambles grew, representing a deep-seated anger towards her childhood friend, Jaya, for a forgotten transgression.

The thorns of these brambles pricked her heart every time memories of Jaya surfaced. The rest of her garden suffered, too; the shadows cast by the brambles stifled the growth of the flowers, depriving them of the light they so craved.

One day, an enlightened monk, Alok, passing through Niranjana, was drawn to Mira's garden. Sensing the disharmony, he inquired about the shadows. Mira, with a heavy heart, narrated her tale of betrayal.

Alok, with eyes that seemed to pierce the fabric of reality, said, "In your garden of emotions, what purpose do these brambles serve?"

"They remind me of my pain," replied Mira.

"And do they not also block the light, hindering the growth of other emotions?" Alok pressed.

Mira contemplated, realizing the truth in Alok's words. The resentment she held was not just a reminder of pain but also a barrier to her happiness.

With newfound determination, she decided to confront her past. She sought out Jaya, and they spoke of that long-ago incident. Tears flowed, misunderstandings were unraveled, and in their reunion, the shadows in Mira's garden began to retreat.

In place of the brambles, a new flower bloomed, one she had never seen before – the Lotus of Forgiveness. It radiated a light so pure it illuminated every corner of her garden, allowing all her emotions to flourish in harmony.

Conclusion:

Our hearts, much like Mira's garden, harbor a myriad of emotions. Clinging to resentment casts shadows over our true essence, limiting our potential. By choosing the path of forgiveness, we not only release the shackles of past hurts but also illuminate the vast landscapes of our souls. The tale of Mira is an ode to the transformative power of letting go, urging us to embrace the light within and around us.

THE CAVERN OF GRUDGES

In the sacred land of Dharmapura, atop its loftiest peak, there existed a cavern known as the Vimukti Cavern. Legend spoke of its mysterious acoustics: utter a word, and it would echo with the wisdom of the ancients.

Nichiren, a humble weaver, found his life entangled like the threads he wove. A betrayal by his childhood confidant, Keshav, left a scar so profound that Nichiren's once melodious loom now resonated with notes of sorrow.

One evening, tormented by relentless memories, Nichiren sought solace in the Vimukti Cavern. Standing amidst its magnificence, he shouted, "Betrayal!"

The cavern, in its arcane manner, echoed back, "Release."

Confounded, Nichiren voiced, "Pain!"

The cavern whispered, "Heal."

With tears glistening, he cried, "Keshav!"

The cavern resonated, "Self."

The echoes weren't mere repetitions but reflections, urging introspection. Nichiren sat, meditating on the cavern's wisdom. He pondered: Was Keshav truly the root of his torment, or was it his own clinging to past wounds? Dawn illuminated the cavern as Nichiren, with newfound clarity, realized that his grudges acted as shackles. In blaming Keshav, he had imprisoned himself within walls of resentment. True freedom lay not in waiting for Keshav's atonement but in his own act of forgiveness.

As the sun ascended, Nichiren, with heart unburdened, descended the peak. He approached Keshav, not with accusations but with understanding. The reunion was one of tears and smiles, a tapestry of human frailties and strengths. With the cavern's wisdom woven into his being, Nichiren's loom sang songs of joy again, creating patterns that told tales of a heart that learned to release, heal, and see the self in the other.

Conclusion:

Much like the universe, the cavern reflects our innermost feelings in ways we often overlook. Holding onto past transgressions ensnares us in a perpetual echo of pain. Nichiren's journey within the Vimukti Cavern serves as a reminder that forgiveness is an inward voyage, where the act of letting go is not a sign of weakness but of profound strength. It challenges us to question: Do we hear only our grievances, or do we listen to the deeper echoes of our soul?

THE UNSEEN CHAINS OF VIPARYAYA VALLEY

In the serene realms of Bodhipradesh, there existed a peculiar valley named Viparyaya. Unlike the other valleys adorned with flowers and trees, Viparyaya was starkly barren but had a distinct allure that attracted many.

Deep in its heart was a colossal stone named the 'Avidya Rock.' Enigmatic and captivating, travelers often felt an irresistible urge to touch it. Yet, upon doing so, they'd find their hands chained to it, unable to move away.

Manish, a sage with profound wisdom, had heard tales of this puzzling valley. Although many cautioned him against visiting, his innate curiosity led him towards the Avidya Rock.

Upon reaching the valley, he observed several individuals chained to the rock, from young adventurers to old monks. They wore expressions of regret and sorrow.

Approaching an elder, Manish inquired, "Venerable one, why are so many bound to this stone?"

The elder, with eyes weighed down by years of longing, replied, "This rock represents our past wrongs and transgressions. Once we touch it, reminiscing our past, we become shackled by our own regrets and resentments, unable to move forward."

Manish, looking deeply into the stone, contemplated its essence. He then gently touched it, and as anticipated, chains appeared, binding him. But instead of panic or sorrow, Manish closed his eyes and whispered, "I forgive myself and release all past transgressions. I embrace the present."

To the astonishment of all, the chains dissolved. Inspired, others began echoing his sentiments, forgiving themselves and those who wronged them. One by one, chains broke, releasing the captive souls.

The once desolate Viparyaya Valley, with every act of forgiveness, began to bloom. Trees sprouted, flowers blossomed, and the Avidya Rock, losing its dominance, became a mere pebble, a testament to the transformed valley.

Conclusion:

Often, we are prisoners not of physical chains but of our own inability to forgive and move past our regrets. The Avidya Rock stands symbolic of these self-imposed bindings. Manish's act is a gentle reminder that the keys to our chains lie within us. Through understanding and forgiveness, we can transform our barren valleys into lush paradises, urging readers to reevaluate the chains they might unknowingly be carrying and find the strength within to release them.

THE SACRED SAGA OF SERENITY

In the remote corners of DharmaYatra, nestled between snow-peaked mountains, lay a hidden gem: the Jharana, a waterfall of shimmering light. While its beauty was unparalleled, it was the legends surrounding the Jharana that drew seekers.

A young scholar named Sayadaw, consumed by past regrets and lingering bitterness, embarked on a pilgrimage to this mystical waterfall, having heard that its waters held the secret to liberation.

Upon arrival, Sayadaw was taken aback by the ethereal aura of the Jharana. It wasn't merely water flowing; it was a cascade of liquid light. The luminous droplets whispered tales of ancient wisdom and universal truths.

Drawn to its magic, Sayadaw cupped the glowing water in her hands, and to her astonishment, each droplet began to murmur words. "*Release,*" one drop whispered. "*Forgive,*" hummed another.

Sayadaw, moved by the experience, sat meditatively by the Jharana, letting the droplets splash upon her. As they did, memories of past wrongs and betrayals emerged. But now, viewed through the prism of the Jharana's wisdom, they looked different.

She recalled a dear friend's betrayal, which once seemed unforgivable. But now, the whispers of the Jharana prompted a deeper inquiry: Was holding onto this resentment serving her? Or had it become a heavy shackle, impeding her spiritual journey?

Each droplet that touched her seemed to cleanse a part of her soul, urging her to see beyond the superficial wounds and recognize the shared humanity and imperfections.

As days turned into nights, Sayadaw's heart, once filled with anguish, began to soften. The weight of the past seemed to dissolve in the sacred waters, replaced by a profound sense of compassion and understanding.

With a heart light and unburdened, Sayadaw departed from the Jharana, not just as a scholar but as a beacon of forgiveness. She realized that in holding onto grudges, one only poisons oneself. True freedom and peace lay in letting go and understanding the transient nature of life's tribulations.

Conclusion:

The Jharana's whispers are emblematic of the timeless wisdom that echoes through the annals of spirituality. Holding onto resentment is like clutching a burning ember, hoping it'll harm another, but it's oneself who gets burnt. Sayadaw's transformation by Jharana's shores implores readers to introspect: Are we drinking from the chalice of bitterness or the elixir of forgiveness? The choice determines the course of our inner pilgrimage.

THE WEIGHTLESS PEBBLE

In the vast plains of Dharmasara, there was a peculiar ritual that people from nearby villages observed. Once a year, during the Festival of Reflection, each individual would journey to the sacred River Anupava, carrying with them a small pebble. This was not just any pebble but one that symbolized a burden they bore: a grudge, an old wound, a festering anger, or lingering guilt.

Priya, a woman known for her wisdom yet weighed down by a hidden sorrow, participated in this ritual every year. Yet, unlike others, her pebble never found its way into the waters of Anupava.

One year, a young monk named Saman observed Priya's ritual. Curious, he approached her, "Venerable Priya, why do you hold onto your pebble year after year? Why not let the waters take it?"

Priya looked at Saman, her eyes a mirror of depths unexplored. "Dear monk, this pebble, as heavy as it may seem, is not mine to cast away."

Saman, puzzled, sat down beside her, "But isn't the purpose of this ritual to unburden ourselves?"

Priya replied, "To cast a pebble into the river, one must first recognize its weight. My pebble symbolizes a wrong I once committed. By holding onto it, I am constantly reminded of my actions and their consequences."

Saman mused, "Isn't forgiveness, especially self-forgiveness, a path to liberation?"

With a soft sigh, Priya confided, "Many moons ago, I acted out of impulse and hurt someone dear. Although I've sought forgiveness, the weight of my action lingers. This pebble reminds me to be compassionate and considerate in every act."

The monk gently responded, "But venerable Priya, by holding onto this pebble, aren't you denying yourself the same compassion you wish to extend to others?"

A silent moment passed, and Priya's eyes shimmered with realization. "Perhaps it's time to understand that true forgiveness is not just for others but also for oneself."

That year, with Saman by her side and the entire universe as her witness, Priya finally released her pebble into the waters of Anupava, letting the river carry away years of self-imposed burdens.

Conclusion:

In our journey through life, we often carry the weight of our actions, past mistakes, or perceived wrongs. Like Priya's pebble, these burdens can anchor us, preventing spiritual growth and inner peace. Yet, as Saman reminds us, true liberation lies in recognizing the weight and choosing to release it. While it's essential to acknowledge our actions and learn from them, it's equally vital to allow ourselves the grace of forgiveness. The story invites readers to reflect upon their own 'pebbles' and challenges them to embrace the transformative power of forgiveness, both for others and oneself.

THE DANCING SHADOWS OF RAYA

Raya was a gifted shadow puppeteer in the quaint village of Karmala. With the mere movement of her fingers, she brought to life tales of warriors, romances, tragedies, and comedies. People from neighboring villages would gather in the moonlit square to be enchanted by her craft.

However, there was one story Raya never told, not even in the secrecy of her own heart — her personal tale of betrayal.

Many years ago, her closest friend, Anila, had wronged her. The nature of this transgression was so profound that it cast a dark shadow over Raya's heart, a shadow darker than any puppet she had ever maneuvered. Over time, the villagers noticed a subtle transformation in Raya's performances. The tales she narrated grew somber, and the once joyful puppeteer now mostly told tragic stories.

A traveling monk named Dilgo, upon hearing of Raya's mesmerizing yet melancholic performances, decided to pay a visit. As Raya's silhouettes danced under the moon, Dilgo sensed the pain behind her craft.

After the performance, he approached her. "Your art speaks of a deep sorrow, Raya. A sorrow not of fictional tales but of lived experiences."

Raya looked away, her pride preventing her from admitting her inner turmoil. "My stories are but reflections of life, Dilgo."

Dilgo, gazing at the disappearing shadows, mused, "But isn't life also a reflection of what lies in our hearts?"

Over the next few days, Dilgo attended every performance, and soon, the two struck a deep bond. Raya eventually found herself recounting her tale of betrayal to the monk. Dilgo listened, not with judgment but with understanding.

"Why do you carry this burden, Raya? Why let a past shadow define your present light?" Dilgo inquired.

"I can't forgive, Dilgo. The pain is too deep. The memories pull me back every time I try to let go," Raya lamented.

Dilgo picked up a puppet, its silhouette dark against the moonlit canvas. "Every shadow needs light to exist, Raya. Instead of focusing on the shadow, why not shift your gaze to the light? Forgiveness isn't about forgetting; it's about changing the direction of your focus."

The profoundness of Dilgo's words resonated with Raya. That night, she performed a different tale, one of love, forgiveness, and rebirth. The shadows danced, not with sorrow but with hope. The village square was alive with laughter and joy once again.

Conclusion:

In the interplay of light and shadow, life unfolds. Raya's journey is a testament to the power of perspective. While hurt and betrayal are inevitable, dwelling on these shadows only deepens their imprint. The challenge lies not in erasing these shadows but in shifting our focus to the light that casts them. Through Dilgo's wisdom, we are reminded that forgiveness is an act of empowerment, a conscious choice to live in the present light rather than past darkness.

THE EMBER'S GLOW

In the serene town of Lysandra, a peculiar ritual took place every year during the winter solstice. People would gather around a colossal bonfire to write down their regrets, animosities, and sorrows on paper, then cast them into the flames. This ceremony, called the Ember's Glow, symbolized the shedding of past burdens and the welcoming of renewal.

Maela, a diligent weaver in Lysandra, never participated. While the town's folk felt lighter with every passing Ember's Glow, Maela's heart became a reservoir of past wounds. She held onto a betrayal that had torn her family apart many years ago. A rift with her brother, Joren, over a misunderstanding had resulted in years of silence.

One winter, as the Ember's Glow approached, an elderly traveler named Elion visited Lysandra. With deep-set eyes that seemed to hold the universe's wisdom, he took a particular interest in Maela's story after observing her reluctance towards the ceremony.

"Why do you hold back from the glow, young weaver?" Elion asked.

"The fire can't burn away real pain," Maela responded, bitterness evident in her voice.

Elion invited Maela for a walk the next morning, leading her to a frozen pond outside the village. He picked up a heavy rock and handed it to Maela.

"Walk with this rock as far as you can," he instructed.

Maela, puzzled but intrigued, obliged. With every step, the rock's weight seemed to increase, making her journey increasingly laborious. After what felt like miles, she finally exclaimed, "I can't carry this any further!"

Elion nodded, "Just as you shouldn't carry the weight of past grudges any further."

Realization dawned upon Maela. The weight of the rock mirrored the heaviness of her unyielding anger and pain.

"But how do I let it go? The past can't be undone," Maela whispered, tears forming.

Elion gently replied, "No, it can't. But the future is yet to be woven. By holding onto old threads, you deny yourself the vibrant patterns yet to come. Forgiveness doesn't rewrite the past, but it does set the course for a brighter tapestry ahead."

That evening, Maela stood hesitantly by the bonfire. With trembling hands, she wrote down her feelings of resentment and cast them into the flames. As the paper turned to ash, she felt an overwhelming sense of release. She was ready to mend the rift with Joren, not for the past but for the possibility of a shared future.

Conclusion:

The Ember's Glow serves as a powerful metaphor for the transformative energy of forgiveness. While memories remain, letting go of the emotions they tether allows space for healing and growth. Like Maela, we sometimes need a tangible reminder of the burdens we unconsciously bear. Her journey challenges the conventional belief that time alone heals wounds, highlighting that active forgiveness is the key to unlocking trapped potential. It prompts introspection: what weights are we carrying, and are we ready to set them ablaze for a brighter tomorrow?

The Power of Gratitude

Gratitude is a transformative practice that can profoundly alter your life. It fosters a deep sense of appreciation, compassion, and connection, making you more attuned to the present moment and enhancing your overall well-being. By understanding and integrating the principles of gratitude from Buddhism, Taoism, and Ikigai, you can cultivate a richer, more fulfilling life. The tales in this chapter illustrate these teachings, providing a roadmap to a life deeply enriched by the power of thankfulness.

Gratitude can change your life in numerous ways. It can shift your perspective, making you more resilient to stress and adversity, and improve your relationships by fostering empathy and reducing negative emotions. From a psychological standpoint, gratitude has been shown to increase happiness, improve mental health, and even enhance physical well-being. By making gratitude a daily practice, you can rewire your brain to focus on the positive aspects of life, leading to lasting changes in how you experience the world.

Gratitude is a complex and multifaceted emotion that involves recognizing and appreciating the positive aspects of life, whether they are significant events or small daily occurrences. It requires an intentional focus on what we have rather than what we lack.

Gratitude has the power to reshape your life by shifting your focus from what's missing to what's already abundant.

Embracing gratitude can boost your mental and physical well-being, strengthen your relationships, and enhance your resilience. When you practice gratitude regularly, you cultivate a more positive outlook, alleviate stress and anxiety, and foster a deeper sense of connection and fulfillment.

Moreover, gratitude promotes a sense of self-worth and self-esteem. When we acknowledge the kindness and support of others, we recognize our value in their lives and the value of their presence in ours. This mutual recognition can lead to a stronger sense of belonging and connectedness, which is crucial for mental health.

Increasing Resilience Through Gratitude

Resilience, the ability to bounce back from adversity, is another area where gratitude has a significant impact. Grateful individuals are more likely to view challenges as opportunities for growth rather than insurmountable obstacles. This positive outlook can foster a sense of empowerment and determination.

Gratitude also promotes a broader perspective on life, allowing individuals to see beyond immediate difficulties and recognize the long-term benefits of their experiences. This mindset can enhance problem-solving abilities and encourage adaptive coping strategies, making individuals more resilient in the face of life's challenges.

Buddhism: The Path of Gratitude

In Buddhism, gratitude (katannuta) is a fundamental aspect of spiritual practice. It helps cultivate mindfulness, compassion, and a peaceful heart. Buddhism teaches that being grateful not only for blessings but also for challenges is essential for growth and understanding.

The Blooms of Thankfulness: This tale illustrates the Buddhist teaching that every circumstance, no matter how challenging, contains a positive seed. Characters learn to see beyond immediate difficulties, cultivating gratitude for the lessons within their struggles. This practice helps develop patience, resilience, and a deeper appreciation for life's complexities. By embracing gratitude, you can transform adversity into an opportunity for growth and inner peace.

Journey to the Heart of Dawn: In this story, characters embark on a journey of self-discovery and gratitude. Through mindful reflection and meditation, they appreciate the interconnectedness of all beings and the impermanence of life. This journey mirrors the Buddhist practice of mindfulness, where being fully present and aware allows for a profound sense of gratitude for each moment. Mindfulness enhances your ability to appreciate the present, reducing stress and increasing overall well-being.

The Songbird's Serenade: This narrative emphasizes the importance of being grateful for small, everyday moments. Characters find joy and peace in the simple act of listening to a songbird's serenade, reflecting the Buddhist teaching that mindfulness and gratitude are deeply intertwined, enhancing our appreciation for the present. By focusing on the present, you can find joy in the simple pleasures of life, improving your mental and emotional health.

Taoism: Harmony and Gratitude

Taoism teaches that living in harmony with the Tao involves recognizing and appreciating the natural flow of life. Gratitude in Taoism is about embracing simplicity and spontaneity, fostering a deep sense of peace and contentment.

The Lioness and the Elephant: In this story, the lioness and the elephant, representing different aspects of strength and gentleness, learn to appreciate each other's qualities. This tale illustrates the Taoist concept of yin and yang, where opposites complement each other to create harmony. Gratitude for these differences fosters a deeper connection and balance, embodying the Taoist ideal of harmonious coexistence. Recognizing and appreciating the strengths in others can improve your relationships and create a more balanced life.

Ikigai: Purpose and Gratitude

Ikigai, the profound Japanese philosophy, leads us on a journey to uncover our true purpose—the very essence that infuses our lives with meaning and joy. Central to this philosophy is the practice of gratitude, which enriches our experience and deepens our sense of fulfillment, ultimately guiding us towards living a purposeful and fulfilling life. Gratitude in Ikigai involves recognizing the value of both achievements and connections with others, leading to a balanced and meaningful existence.

The Oasis of Appreciation: This tale is a reflection of Ikigai, where characters learn to find gratitude in their daily routines and interactions. By focusing on their passions and contributions, they discover a deeper sense of purpose and contentment. This story highlights that living with purpose involves continuous appreciation for the journey and the people we encounter along the way. By aligning your actions with your passions and values, you can enhance your sense of purpose and satisfaction in life.

THE BLOOMS OF THANKFULNESS

In the realm of celestial realms and sacred whispers rested a secluded hamlet named Sestina, cocooned within the folds of the mountain's embrace. Here, a symphony of laughter and chatter resonated as a gentle reminder of the universal harmony. However, amidst the harmonious existence, there lingered an unspoken sorrow, a melancholy birthed from the absence of the radiant Sun.

In Sestina, the ethereal being named Aria, guardian of the winds, resided. Aria was endowed with the wisdom of the ages and the sanctity of the breezes. A celestial paradox, her essence whispered secrets of unseen worlds yet unseen, her form hidden within the embrace of the ether, obscured by the sorrow enveloping the hamlet.

One day, a wanderer named Seraphim, burdened by the shadows of unfulfilled desires and silenced dreams, wandered into Sestina, his soul yearning for the essence of light.

Seraphim, caught in the entwining threads of worldly worries and transient treasures, sought Aria's ancient wisdom to discover the path to the radiant Sun, the harbinger of life's true treasures.

"O gentle whisperer of the unseen winds, how might a mere mortal uncover the golden rays hidden within the realm of shadows, illuminating the path to life's timeless treasures?" Seraphim inquired, his voice a harmonious blend of hope and despair.

Aria, with her ethereal whispers, painted a tapestry of words in the winds, "The path to the radiant Sun lies not in the pursuit of shadows but in the cultivation of the blooms of thankfulness within one's soul. It is the seeds of gratitude when watered with love and tenderness, that blossom into the radiant Sun, illuminating the unseen, unspoken realms of existence."

Seraphim, his soul dancing to the rhythm of Aria's celestial symphony, embarked on a journey within, sowing the seeds of gratitude within the soil of his being, whispering thanks to the winds for the unseen blessings and silent miracles. He learned to see the unseen beauty within every shadow, to hear the unspoken symphony within every silence, to feel the unseen touch of the divine within every breeze.

With every bloom of thankfulness, the shadows within Seraphim's soul began to dissolve, revealing the radiant Sun hidden within the folds of his being. The hamlet of Sestina, bathed in the golden rays of the uncovered Sun, sang the symphony of the unseen, the unspoken realms becoming the harmonious dance of existence.

Conclusion:

The Blooms of Thankfulness serves as a delicate reminder of the transformative, illuminative power of gratitude. It is not the pursuit of transient treasures but the cultivation of thankfulness that reveals the true, unseen treasures of existence. This tale invites us to delve deeper into our beings, to uncover the radiant Sun within, to illuminate the unseen, to dance to the unspoken symphony of the universe. It is a gentle whisper to our souls to cultivate the blooms of thankfulness, to see the unseen, to hear the unspoken, to feel the unseen touch of the divine within every moment of existence, to transform our perceptions, and to embrace the radiant dance of life.

JOURNEY TO THE HEART OF DAWN

In the heart of a serene village called Kunga, where the rivers flowed with gentle whispers and the trees danced to nature's rhythm, there was a profound stillness. The villagers, each skilled in their craft and united in their pursuit of daily life, found themselves chained by a growing restlessness. An invisible fog of discontent had descended upon Kunga, causing its inhabitants to question their life's meaning.

In the midst of this collective turmoil, Ananda, a young villager, felt the weight of this unspoken distress more than others. Every evening, he would sit by the riverside, gazing at the setting sun, pondering on the source of this pervasive emptiness.

One day, a sage named Paramitan arrived in Kunga. Word quickly spread about the wise sage who spoke of worlds beyond the visible, of truths that pierced the veils of everyday life. Seeking clarity, Ananda approached Paramitan with a heavy heart.

"Why do we feel this void, this insatiable longing, even amidst abundance?" Ananda questioned.

Paramitan, gazing deeply into the horizon, replied, "You seek the nectar of fulfillment not in the vastness of the universe but in the confinements of desire. Begin a journey, not of miles, but of moments. Seek the power of gratitude, for it is the bridge between the world of longing and the realm of fulfillment."

Intrigued and inspired, Ananda decided to embark on this suggested journey. Every day, he would find a moment, an incident, or an entity to express his gratitude towards. From the smallest pebble to the vast sky, Ananda whispered words of thanks.

As days turned into weeks, a transformation began to blossom within him. The trees seemed greener, the river's song sweeter, and the wind's embrace warmer. The void that once consumed him was now being replaced with a profound sense of contentment. The fog of discontent began to lift, not just for Ananda but for all of Kunga.

Months later, the village was transformed. The rivers sang songs of joy, and every breeze carried whispers of gratitude.

Kunga, once clouded by discontent, now shimmered in the radiant glow of thankfulness.

Conclusion:

The tale of Kunga teaches us the boundless power of gratitude. In our relentless quest for more, we often overlook the abundance that already graces our lives. Gratitude is not merely an act but a transformative force capable of illuminating the darkest corners of our existence. It challenges our conventional approach to happiness, suggesting that joy doesn't stem from acquiring more but from deeply appreciating what we already possess. As Ananda discovered, the journey to fulfillment lies not in the distance covered but in the depth of our gratitude.

THE SONGBIRD'S SERENADE

In the heart of the dense, vibrant Jungalaya forest, where every leaf whispered tales of old and the wind danced to the songs of time, lived animals of all shapes and sizes. They were bound by an unspoken law of the jungle - survival. Yet, amidst the competition and occasional skirmishes, there was an undercurrent of respect and acknowledgment of the intricate web of life they all were a part of.

Nalanda, a young songbird with iridescent blue feathers, was known far and wide for her melodious songs that welcomed every dawn. However, she harbored a silent sorrow. While every animal praised her for her melodies, she felt her songs were incomplete. This sorrow led her to sing less and less, which cast a quiet gloom over Jungalaya.

One day, while perched on her favorite banyan tree branch, she watched a seemingly insignificant scene unfold beneath her. An old tortoise, Rangjung, slowly made her way to the riverbank. Behind her, she left a trail that made it easier for other animals to traverse. Nalanda noticed how animals, big and small, expressed silent gratitude towards Rangjung, not with words but through acts. The squirrel would drop nuts near Rangjung's path, the deer would keep a protective eye when she rested, and the butterfly would often accompany her, providing her with a dance of colors to enjoy.

Nalanda approached Rangjung and asked, "Why do you do this, making paths, even though it makes your journey longer and harder?"

Rangjung, with her ancient eyes that held stories of many monsoons, replied, "Little bird, life has given me a sturdy shell and a patient heart. This is my way of expressing gratitude for what I have by giving back. And in their own ways, they all express their gratitude back. It's a silent dance of give and take, young one."

Inspired, Nalanda realized her songs weren't just for her but were her gift to Jungalaya. Her sorrow wasn't in her songs but in her inability to see the gratitude the forest showed her. She began singing again, this time not seeking appreciation but as an expression of her gratitude for the life, the forest, and the daily miracles around her.

The forest awakened once more, bathed in the melodies of gratitude. Animals began to recognize and appreciate the little things others did for them. The once survival-driven Jungalaya transformed into a sanctuary of mutual respect and gratitude, all inspired by a songbird's silent serenade.

Conclusion:

Gratitude is not just an emotion but a transformative force. It's not always expressed in words but often in subtle gestures, a silent acknowledgment, a simple act. Like Nalanda, once we shift our perspective to view life through the lens of gratitude, we not only find our song but also realize that the world dances along, reciprocating in its unique way. Every act of kindness, no matter how small, ripples through the vast ocean of existence, touching souls and making the universe a harmonious place.

THE OASIS OF APPRECIATION

In the tranquil groves of Anandavana, life thrived in silent symbiosis. The animals lived in a dance of balance, where each step taken was a testimony to a shared understanding of existence. But, as in any realm, the mundane sometimes overshadows the extraordinary.

Meera, a graceful doe with eyes that mirrored the depths of the forest ponds, was admired for her beauty and agility. However, Meera was constantly tormented by a persistent feeling of inadequacy. She envied the birds for their freedom to soar, the fish for their shimmering scales, and the mighty elephant for his strength. She believed her existence was mundane in comparison.

One evening, a grand assembly was held under the ancient Wisdom Tree, where animals gathered to share tales and songs. Meera lost in her thoughts, was interrupted by the soft voice of an aged tortoise, Mohan.

"I've witnessed countless seasons," Mohan began, "and in all these years, I've observed the beauty of gratitude. Today, I wish to share a tale that may seem ordinary but holds within it the essence of our forest."

He recounted how, during a particularly harsh summer, the river had almost dried up. The animals were filled with despair. It was then that Meera, with her keen sense of hearing, had detected the faint sound of a trickling stream, leading them to a hidden waterfall. The animals rejoiced, and the forest was saved.

"But, dear Meera," Mohan continued, looking into her eyes, "do you remember what you said back then?"

Meera blinked, recollecting, "I only said that I was fortunate to have heard it."

Mohan nodded, "And that, dear one, is the power of gratitude. You didn't claim the discovery as a testament to your prowess. Instead, you were grateful for your gift and used it for the greater good. That is why, even years later, every time an animal drinks from that stream, they send silent waves of gratitude your way. It's in the squirrel's twitching tail, the butterfly's gentle flutter, and in the elephant's trumpeting joy."

Meera's eyes glistened with understanding. She realized that her worth wasn't defined by envying the gifts of others but by recognizing and being grateful for her own. She may not fly like the birds or shimmer like the fish, but her unique gift had once saved the forest.

Conclusion:

Gratitude isn't always about grand gestures. It's in the silent acknowledgments, the unspoken thanks, the gentle nods of appreciation. When we shift from a mindset of comparison to one of gratitude, we recognize the profound impact of our unique existence. We begin to see that our purpose is intertwined with the silent thanks we receive and give every day. And in this tapestry of silent gratitude, we find our true place in the vast expanse of life, where every small moment of appreciation becomes a thread connecting us to the larger story of humanity. It is in these quiet acts that we create ripples of kindness, shaping not just our own experience, but also the collective experience of those around us.

THE LIONESS AND THE ELEPHANT

In the vast plains of the Serengeti, where the golden grasslands touched the azure sky, a tale unfolded, whispered by the winds and echoed by the savannah's inhabitants.

Mila, a young and radiant lioness, found herself troubled. She was the fiercest of her pride, an unmatched hunter with strength and prowess that commanded respect. But with each passing day, a growing restlessness consumed her. Every success, every hunt, seemed to accentuate an emptiness that grew within her.

One day, as the sun painted the horizon in hues of crimson and amber, Mila sought out Rafiki, the wise old elephant known to possess knowledge as vast as the stars themselves. "Why," Mila lamented, "despite all I've achieved and all I command, do I still feel incomplete?"

Drawing upon the wisdom of ages, Rafiki beckoned Mila to a secluded glen. Here, a radiant pond mirrored the heavens above. The old elephant instructed Mila to gaze into the waters and describe what she saw.

"I see my reflection," she observed, noting her strong physique and magnificent mane.

"But what else do you see, young lioness?"

Looking deeper, Mila began to recognize other shapes— swirls of fish that danced below the surface, the shimmering leaves of overhanging trees, and the gentle ripples caused by a drinking gazelle. "I see...life. An interwoven tapestry of it."

Rafiki nodded, "The power you seek, the fulfillment, doesn't come from your accomplishments alone. It emanates from gratitude. Gratitude for the smaller moments, the unsung heroes in your story - the gazelles that sustain you, the trees that provide shade, the waters that quench your thirst."

Mila pondered this, her gaze drifting to a nearby nest where a bird was feeding its young. The tiny creatures chirped in joy, expressing their gratitude in pure, unadulterated song.

The lioness turned to Rafiki, realization dawning upon her. "To be grateful is to recognize every strand of kindness, every touch of beauty, even in the mundane. It's to understand that my strength is not mine alone but is woven from the threads of all that surrounds and supports me."

Rafiki smiled, his eyes twinkling with ancient wisdom. "To truly roar, one must first learn to sing. Sing the song of gratitude."

From that day, Mila wasn't just the pride's fiercest lioness but also its most grateful. Her roars echoed with strength, but her purrs told stories of love, gratitude, and the intricate ballet of life that danced around her.

Conclusion:

The tale of Mila teaches us that in the heart of our pursuits, it is easy to overlook the myriad of blessings that construct our journey. Though commendable, power, success, and strength become truly meaningful when coupled with gratitude. To acknowledge and be thankful for the interdependencies of life is to embrace an expanded sense of self - one that is richer, deeper, and infinitely more connected. In all its wild beauty, the Serengeti serves as a mirror, reflecting the interconnected tapestry of our lives and the myriad reasons we have to be grateful.

Final Words of Thanks

Thank you for exploring the stories and reflections within these pages. Whether you've found wisdom in the parables, solace in the tales of compassion, or inspiration in the journey toward balance and understanding, I hope this book has been a meaningful companion on your path.

Perhaps the narratives have sparked a moment of introspection or offered a fresh perspective on life's challenges and joys. If these stories have touched you, your thoughts could serve as a guiding light for others contemplating their own journey of growth and discovery.

Your reflections and experiences, if shared, might encourage fellow readers to dive into the teachings woven throughout this book. Consider leaving your thoughts and impressions—they are invaluable in helping others decide to take this step.

Thank you for allowing these stories to become a part of your world. May they continue to inspire and guide you, fostering a deeper connection to yourself and the world around you.

Walk forward with kindness, wisdom, and peace as your companions, one story at a time.

If you'd like to share your feedback, scan the QR code below.

Printed in Great Britain
by Amazon

61130648R00167